Attituae of Gratitude

Kennedy

Attitude of Gratitude

The Life of Wilfred Watson

By
Virginia G. Tait

*If ye then be risen with Christ,
seek those things which are above,
where Christ sitteth on the right hand of God.
Set your affection on things above,
not on things on the earth.
For ye are dead,
and your life is hid with Christ in God.*

Colossians 3:1-3

**Redeemer
✝✝✝ Books**

Attitude of Gratitude

Copyright © 1992 Virginia G. Tait

All rights reserved. No part of this book or accompanying audio tape recording may be reproduced or transmitted in any form or by any means, electronic or mechanical, including photocopying, recording, or any information storage and retrieval system without written permission.

Redeemer ISBN 1-877607-56-8
WEC ISBN 0-900828-56-0

Published by Redeemer Books
P.O. Box 15
Winamac, Indiana, USA

Book published jointly with WEC Publications,
Bulstrode, Gerrards Cross, Bucks. SL9 8SZ, England.

Books may be obtained from:
Bulstrode, Gerrards Cross, Bucks. SL9 8SZ, England.
Box 1707, Fort Washington, PA 19034-8707, USA
37 Aberdeen Avenue, Hamilton, ONT. L8P 2N6, Canada
Box 1154, Three Hills, Alberta, T0M 2A0, Canada

Audio version and books obtainable from:
Attitude of Gratitude, 10627 S. Church St.,Chicago, IL 60643-2909

Library of Congress Cataloging-in-Publication Data

Tait, Virginia G., 1927-
   Attitude of Gratitude : the life of Wilfred Watson / by Virginia G. Tait.
    p. cm.
   Includes bibliographical references.
   ISBN 1-877607-56-8
   1. Watson, Wilfred, 1914-   . 2. Missionaries--South America--Biography.
3. Missionaries--Canada--Biography. I. Title.
BV2852.W38T35   1992
266' .0092--dc20
[B]   92-25808
                                                                            CIP

Endorsements

Trained at Prairie Bible Institute, Wilfred was "bitten by the bug of missions" and in 1939 went to South America, with the faith mission, WEC. His story has been one of evangelism, church planting, and Bible teaching, often amid incredible circumstances of fanatical opposition and physical hardship.

Our young people today desperately need heroes—models of what it means to be committed utterly to the Lord Jesus Christ. Give them this book, *Attitude of Gratitude*, and let it inspire a new generation of missionaries to serve the hidden and lost peoples of our planet.

Dr. Ted S. Rendall
Chancellor of Prairie Bible Institute

Wilf was the missionary I most wanted to be like. He is the most versatile missionary I know. He proved to be a good pastor in several churches and was much in demand for evangelistic campaigns. I have never listened to anyone who could control an audience so well. He told the most appropriate stories possible. Sometimes his words brought tears; often they were rib ticklers. He was the favorite speaker at youth camps, retreats, etc.

He loved to take his turn at our Christian Training Center. He rarely finished the material for the course but his enthusiasm for the Word always outshone any lack of completion of a study.

His musical ability was much appreciated. He played his accordion with much feeling, singing out with joy sparkling in his eyes.

At one of our yearly conferences he lead us in the observance of the Lord's Supper. Later, three of the missionaries commented that it was the most impressive service they had ever attended. They asked me how much time he had to prepare for it. I had only mentioned it to him a short while before, but I knew he was always ready to preach, teach, lead, sing, pray, counsel, encourage or whatever the need of the moment might be. Wilf was a brother, a colleague, a model, a friend.

Jim Davidson—SAM field leader in Bolivia

Wilfred and Elizabeth were a great encouragement to Bob and me during our first two years of missionary service. Through the years their lives have been an inspiration and a challenge to us.

Wilda (Mrs. Robert) Savage—TEAM and HCJB

"'He persisted as one who was constantly seeing Him who can't be seen...' (Heb. 11:27, Beck Version) written of Moses, can also be said of Wilf Watson. It is the only adequate explanation for the exploits of this missionary to Peace River country, Colombia, Venezuela, Bolivia, and Latins in Vancouver. We of the North American leadership team marvel at the effectiveness of his representation of WEC International in U.S.A. and Canada, even in his late seventies."

Elwin Palmer—WEC leader

"Mom and Pop Watson taught me how to be a missionary. Everything was strange and frightening to me. My husband, Robert, was raised in a missionary family in South America and was doing OK, but everything was strange and frightening to me. Mom Watson's stories emboldened me. With her and Pop's advice and encouragement, I decided that *I* could go on the bus to market and get out and mingle with the people. They taught me to have an open door to my neighbors, and to minister to the people."

Carol (Mrs. Robert) Evaul—SAM missionary

(Carol Evaul, who drew the unsigned pictures for the book, met the Watsons after her first few months in Bolivia.)

ABOUT THE AUTHOR

The author Virginia G. Tait is a close friend and former co-worker of Wilfred and Elizabeth Watson. For ten years she taught missionary children (including their daughter, Florence) and assisted in Christian schools in South America. For 21 years she taught bilingually in a Chicago public school.

She attended Prairie Bible Institute (13 years after Mr. Watson did) and earned a B. Educ. and M.S. in Urban Education, both from Chicago State University. Chicago has always been her family home.

CONTENTS

Acknowledgements	xi
Introduction	xiii
I. Preparation for Missionary Service:	
Alberta, 1914-1938	1
Foolishness is Bound in the Heart of a Child	1
The Way of a Man with a Maid	2
The Trapped Rabbit	3
The Light Shines in the Darkness	3
All Things Become New	6
Weeping May Endure for a Night	7
But Joy Comes in the Morning	8
In Everything Give Thanks	10
God Works in All Things for Good	10
Sowing Seeds of Righteousness	12
God Supplies All Needs	15
II. Initiation to the Mission Field: Colombia, 1939-1942	21
Content with What You Have	21
With Stammering Lips and Another Tongue he Speaks ...	21
Serving the Lord with Gladness	24
How Good and How Pleasant to Dwell Together in Unity!	25
III. Teaming up for Missionary Service:	
in Northern Colombia and Venezuela, 1942-1954	29
It Is Not Good That Man Should Be Alone	29
Two Are Better than One	35
Whoever Loses His Life for My Sake, Shall Find It	39
The Angel of the Lord Encamps Around	
Them That Fear Him	42
I Will Make You Fishers of Men	46
Persecuted for Righteousness Sake	47
Accepting Joyfully the Seizure of Property	51
Watering and Reaping	52
Bread Cast upon the Waters, Found	53
God Gave Them Another Heart	54
The Angel Said, "Follow Me"	55
The Spread of the "Missionary Rabies"	56
Children Are a Heritage from the Lord	58

IV. Restoration to WEC: Venezuela and Colombia, 1954-1970   61
    The Lost Ax Head   61
    The Ax Head Restored   65
    A Gem Sparkles in the Desert   67
    I Have Set Before You an Open Door   70
    God Glorified in Sacrificial Love   72
    They That Feared the Lord Spoke Often One to Another   77
    What God has Joined Together   78
    Disciples, Baptized and Living Godly Lives   79
    Hospitality Guajibo Style   81
    All Your Children Shall Be Taught of the Lord   82
    Prosperity and Good Health   85
    He Owns the Cattle...   87
    Heartbreaks   89

V. Representing WEC: USA, 1970-1978   93
    He Heals the Brokenhearted   93
    God's Thoughts Are Not Wilf's Thoughts   93
    God Gives Grace and a Home   94
    Opening Doors for WEC   95
    Rendering to Caesar   96

VI. Church planting and development:
    Vancouver and Bolivia: 1978---   101
    Knowing How to Abound   101
    ...And thy House   102
    In Season, Out of Season   103
    Pruning, Nurturing, and Growing   104
    To Everything There is a Time   106
    Vision Correctly Focused   107
    In Perils of Robbers   109
    The Windows of Heaven Opened   110
    It Is the Lord That Heals   112
    Hinderance brings Increase   115
    Biking to Paradise   117
    Traveling without Class   118
    Dynamic Teaching at CCC   119
    Christ is Magnified   120
    Good News from Bolivia   122
    Relatives, Citizenship, and Travel   122
    Sitting Where They Sat   123
    Continuing Challenges for the Septuagenarians   129

CONTENTS ix

Memories of my Dad by Eric Watson	133
Epilogue: Sonship, not Servanthood by Wilfred Watson	134
Bibliography	137
Glossary of Spanish Names and Places:	139
Maps	143

ILLUSTRATIONS AND MAPS

"He played his accordion..."	xiv
"Dear Lord Jesus...I'm a wicked sinner..."	4
"No tiene papá."	23
United for Christ	36
"These people have a right to live!"	44
Abounding and being abased in the Castle	64
"This is my Daddy"	76
"What is that syllable?"	84
Diagram of Emaús	84
Polly wants to evangelize	86
"The blood of Jesus Christ cleanses us from all sin."	116
Map of Alberta, Canada	143
Map of Colombia and Venezuela	144
Map of Bolivia and South America	145
Map of USA	146

Acknowledgements

"Gratitude unexpressed," Brother Watson told me, "is ingratitude." I want to express my gratitude to my Lord, Jesus Christ, who commissioned me to put together this biography of my long-time friends, Wilfred Watson and his wife, Elizabeth. Repeated confirmations have affirmed God's leading in this labor of love.

Wilfred and Elizabeth Watson contributed the bulk of the material: his letters written to and saved by his beloved Sunday School teacher, Lem Fowler (who went to be with the Lord early this year), form letters collected by Bobbie Johnstone, stories told on tapes, and conversations. Mr. and Mrs. Watson have been an unending source of encouragement.

Dr. Wesley Nelson initiated the project and collected the above materials plus letters from some of Mr. Watson's friends and former coworkers. He offered guidance as I wrote, and reviewed the manuscript with me. Mrs. Nelson undertook the mammoth task of transcribing the tapes. Together they have been a great encouragement to me.

Reverend Watson's family, friends, and former co-workers have been most helpful. I checked with almost every available person mentioned in the book. They gave enthusiastic approval to the stories connected with them—after making their changes and additions.

Early encouragement came from my dear Mother who, in her hundredth year, listened attentively to the tapes as I proofread the transcriptions. It was her final labor of love. My entire family has been most encouraging.

The Oak Lawn Alliance Church has been a constant source of encouragement and prayer support. The children listened enthusiastically to the stories, asking questions that prompted clarification in the book. When I told about Pastor Watson taking a lady and her children in the cab of his truck five miles in the desert country of Venezuela, one boy asked about seat belts. I had to explain that in 1960 in an area where he *might* encounter another vehicle in a week of driving, seat belts were not an issue.

I am most grateful to all who proofread and reviewed the manuscript, including my sister Ruth Morrison, my neighbor Frances Phillips, my friend Becki Pierce, and WEC friends—Elwin Palmer and Hellen Kuleskey. Jean Levy, Gary Wilkens, and Ella Lindvall checked the first half of the book, each one approaching it from a different perspective.

Artists Carol Evaul, SAM missionary to Bolivia, and Judy Summers of WEC worked long and lovingly on the book. Carol did the line drawings; Judy did the drawing of Camp Hill and the other art work.

Friends of the Watsons have graciously granted permission to quote from their works which are described in the bibliography: Elof Anderson, Stephen E. Savage, Sophie Muller, and the widow of Washington Padilla.

To each of the above I give my hearty thanks, and to all of you who told me you were looking forward to the publishing of this book, and assured me that you would read it.

Virginia G. Tait
July, 1992

Introduction

Wilfred Watson and his wife had ample excuse for complaining during times of poverty, persecution, losses, disappointments, frustrations, excruciatingly painful travel, and difficult living situations. But they chose the opposite of complaining: an attitude of gratitude. As a youth in his home province of Alberta, Canada, during their missionary career in South America, and in representing their mission Wilfred and Elizabeth Watson chose to set their affections on things above rather than on material things, and lived out their life verses, Colossians 3:1-3.

Most of their lives the Watsons have rejoiced to be part of the Worldwide Evangelization Crusade, recently renamed WEC International. The first ten years of their married life they worked with The Evangelical Alliance Mission (TEAM), Elizabeth's mission. They greatly appreciated TEAM and maintained close ties and good fellowship after returning to WEC, the mission with which Wilfred had begun his foreign service. At normal retirement time they founded a Latino church in Canada. The next decade they delighted in rugged missionary work in Bolivia with the South America Mission (SAM).

Wilf put into practice that which he learned as a WEC candidate: be always ready to preach, pray, or die. As he "died to self" and put high priority on prayer, God gave him much opportunity for every variety of preaching.

This book has been written by an American, but we expect it to be read by people of many countries. Therefore we have translated our measurements to the metric system. However, we have kept the money in dollars and cents. Over the years, money in Canada and the United States has been roughly equivalent. American spelling has been used throughout.

Attitude of Gratitude is available in both print and audio cassette form. Open yourself to the challenge, excitement, and blessing of living a life "hid with Christ in God." Give the book or tape to young people who are making life's decisions. Share it with children and teens who are forming life's attitudes and habits.

"He played his accordion with much feeling, singing out with much joy sparkling in his eyes."

Chapter I

PREPARATION FOR MISSIONARY SERVICE: ALBERTA, 1914-1938

Foolishness Is Bound in the Heart of a Child　　　*Proverbs 22:15*

The pugnacious, eight year-old toughy generated chaos! Parents and teachers agreed that something had to be done. The solution: Sunday School!

Wilfred hated Sunday School. In that detested formal setting he was taught that good children go to heaven but bad ones go to another place. He knew he was probably a candidate for the place of the wicked, but to preclude any danger that he might accompany the goody-goodies, he tried to be a bit worse than he might otherwise have been. He wanted a wide margin to be sure to be with his kind.

Compounding the misery, he had to submit to a thorough scrubbing and best clothes before being sent to Sunday School. It was the worst hour of the week—even worse than school.

One Sunday, all decked out, Wilf encountered a baseball game. "Com'on and play with us," called the guys.

"Can't. Gotta go to Sunday School."

"Sunday School? That's for sissies!"

Hating Sunday School and loving baseball, Wilfred threw off his coat. Out to third base bounded the truant!

The clock struck four. Sunday School was over. Dusting off his clothes and patting his wayward blond hair, Wilfred started home whistling, "Yes, Jesus loves me."

"Where've you been, Boy?"

"Sunday School, Dad."

"No, you haven't. Your sisters said you didn't go to Sunday School. Where is the little picture card they always give you?"

Thinking fast he continued lying. "I was a missionary. On the way home I saw a little boy who didn't go to Sunday School so I gave him my pretty picture."

"You come here!"

After the worst licking of his life, Wilfred was sent to bed without supper where he lay talking to the walls: "When I get big, I'll *never* go to church. I *hate* Sunday School. I *hate* church. I *hate* my parents. I *hate* my Sunday School teacher. I *hate* preachers. I'll *never* go back!"

Under protest, he continued to attend. The longer he endured, the more he loathed it. One day the angry, belligerent lad would love all he had previously abhorred, but that was in the unforeseeable future.

The Way of a Man with a Maid   *Proverbs 30:19*

Wilfred's father, Tom Watson, was the youngest of six children. His older sisters helped the housekeeper and father raise him after the early death of their mother. When a step-mother entered the family, the teenager was sent from England to western Canada. There, on his uncle's farm, he labored for a small stipend without opportunity to continue his education.

At age seventeen he claimed a "loser" homestead near Cereal in southeastern Alberta (See map of Alberta, p.146). Summers he cleared and coaxed the land; winters he hauled dirt with his horse and mule for the Grand Trunk Railway.

Several years later his correspondence with England informed him a buddy had died, leaving a girlfriend, Florence Sanderson. Tom remembered her from his childhood work of delivering milk before and after school. He initiated a correspondence with the reluctant maiden who refused to venture to Canada to marry a man whom she did not remember and might not even like.

Tom saved his money and, after nine years of homesteading, headed east. Rather than deplete his savings, he escorted cattle by train and ship across Canada and the Atlantic. Arriving at Yorkshire, England, he was met by Florence and her father who *did* remember him as a youth.

That winter the music-loving swain wooed and won the petite songster, daughter of a godly Baptist Sunday School Superintendent. The romance that began by mail climaxed with an Easter Monday wedding, March 24, 1913.

The voyage to America, 21 days of severe sea-sickness, nearly drained the life from the tiny bride. Travel across Canada brought the delicate city girl to an old sod shanty on the plains—the biggest shock of her life. The following May, Wilfred was born and after another 14 months, Liela arrived. The unproductive farm wore down the lonely little mother but, with World War I raging in Europe, she feared that if her husband left it, he might be drafted. So, she bit her lip and sang the songs of her girlhood.

After the Armistice and at the advice of his farming pal—an alcoholic doctor—Tom left the homestead for town work in the lumber yards.

After Muriel was born, he headed west for the growing city of Calgary and rented a two-room apartment, then sent for Florence and the three preschoolers. Although Tom worked diligently 60 hours a week, his wife found the 30¢ an hour wage didn't cover her choice of food, much less any luxuries, telephone, or even a nickel to ride the street car.

The Trapped Rabbit

In 1924 the Watsons moved to a four-room house. For Wilfred, the best part of the move was that it was too far to go to Sunday School. The next best part was the red-headed neighbor, Mike, whom Wilf pitied because his sister had recently drowned. She had been sent to the river for water when their's was cut off and the current had dragged her in. The two boys became fast friends, playing together all week—without the threat of Sunday School.

That first Sunday afternoon Mike stunned Wilfred with, "Oh! It's time for Sunday School."

"Man, I thought you were a keen guy, but if you go to Sunday School, you're no friend of mine."

"We have fun in Sunday School. I go every Sunday."

"You're not going to find me cleaning up for that!"

"No one gets cleaned up. We go just as we are."

"With toes sticking out of our shoes?"

"Sure. Just like this. Com'on! We have lots of fun!"

Reluctantly Wilfred conceded, feeling like a trapped rabbit.

The Light Shines in the Darkness   II Corinthians 4:6

At the city mission, Wilfred joined the lusty singing and truly enjoyed it: "I've got the joy, joy, joy, joy down in my heart," "Dare to be a Daniel...." Then, to a tiny, windowless cellar room the youthful song leader, Mr. Lem Fowler, herded a pack of rowdies. Out came his Bible and Wilf steeled himself to hear the words: "If you're good boys and go to Sunday School, you'll go to heaven and if you're bad, you'll go where the bad boys go."

But no! The visitor felt Mr. Fowler's penetrating eyes: "You're a bad bunch of rascals! You're as lost as a duck on ice! If you don't let the Lord Jesus Christ come into your heart and save you, you're all lost." Never had Wilfred heard such a gospel presentation.

Dear Lord Jesus ... I'm a wicked sinner...

After class, Wilf saw the teacher approaching him. "You're new here, aren't you? Did you like it? Will you come again next week?" Wilfred answered, "Yes, Sir," to each question. Then Mr. Fowler amazed him with, "Would you like to ask your mama if you could go home with me for supper next Sunday? I'll take you on my bicycle after Sunday School and then to your house after supper."

It was an excited lad who raced home. "Mother, Mother! Can I go to the mission Sunday School next Sunday? My teacher wants to take me home for supper afterwards."

"Yes, you can go. Beat it."

"It's not now. It's next Sunday."

Suddenly alert, his mother whirled around. "Where have you been?"

"To Sunday School."

"Dressed like that?"

"They were all like this. But can I go?"

Bewildered, Florence watched her eagerly impatient rascal count the days of the longest week of his life. She almost fainted when he announced, "Mom, I'm going to Sunday School." He submitted to the scrubbing of his neck, the removal of dirt from his ears, and even the donning of his best clothes.

The singing was fantastic; the lesson great. But best of all, Mr. Fowler remembered the invitation! The bar of that bike might have been a cushioned limousine seat for all Wilfred cared!

Entering the two-story frame house, Wilfred met the mother. As she put the meal on the table, her son led Wilf into the parlor. Pulling a black book from his shirt pocket and opening to John 3:16, he asked, "Can you read this verse, Son?"

Hesitantly the little fellow read, "For God so loved the world that he gave his only be-be-begotten Son that who-that who-whosoever believeth in him should not perish but have ev-ever-everlasting life."

Mr. Fowler repeated it. "You don't want to perish, do you?"

"No, Sir."

"Would you like to have everlasting life?"

"Yes, Sir." Wilfred was interested. He listened to the full explanation of the verse.

Then Mr. Fowler asked, "Would you like to believe in the Lord Jesus as your Savior, the One who died for you, so that you'll have everlasting life and never perish?" Wilfred did! As they knelt together, the teacher prayed and the child repeated phrase by phrase: "Dear Lord Jesus...I'm a wicked sinner..." (He remembered stealing candy and the police being called in.) "I don't want to perish...but I believe that Jesus is my Savior...Thank You for saving me...in Jesus name, amen."

The sun was still bright in the evening sky when Wilf burst into his four-room house with gala tales of the bike rides and supper with the Fowlers! Little did the ten-year-old imagine the blessing and excitement that would follow.

All Things Become New   II Corinthians 5:17

The next morning when Wilfred went out to play he noticed the Jewish boy who lived across the street loitering in front of the Watson home. Wilf wasn't just anti-Semitic; he was anti-everyone. He yelled at Abie, "You get over on the other side of the street, where you belong, you Jew Abie."

Doubling up his fist Wilfred positioned himself to strike a punch when he heard a strange voice: "You don't do that anymore."

"Who said that?" Seeing no one, he boasted, "I'm not scared of that Jew boy," and again aimed a blow at him.

The second time he heard, "You don't do that anymore."

Instead of punching him, Wilf stepped over and hugged Abie—who was more scared than ever. Abie knew something was different. Wilfred knew it, too. Jesus was in his life.

His new life extended to his family. "Come on, Liela! Let's go to Sunday School. And you do what I did last week, OK?" The "almost twin," a year younger but the same size, accompanied her brother-pal to the mission. He introduced her to Mr. Fowler and asked him to tell her, too, how to be saved. That afternoon Liela accepted the Lord as her Savior. What joy that brought to the little missionary!

Wilfred couldn't be kept away from the mission after that. He began to realize his attitudes were changing. His heart was stirred as he saw missionary pictures of semi-naked, primitive Brazilian Indians without Christ, without hope. For the next 15 years he prayed every day that God would help him to be a missionary in South America. The longer he prayed, the more unlikely it seemed that he could ever realize his dream.

In the meantime, missionary preparation included witnessing to pals and becoming an obedient son and student. With others from the mission, he participated in street meetings. On a corner vacant lot with a soap-box, 13-year-old Wilfred told the crowds how he had come to know Jesus as his Savior, and how the Lord had changed his life. During those depression years the streets were teeming with homeless people, such as men who had traveled by freight train and jumped off the cars in Calgary. Their hearts were hungry and scores followed Wilfred and his friends into the mission where many came to know the Lord.

Although his parents rarely attended services, they did appreciate the change in their son and permitted his sisters to accompany him to the mission. Also they yielded to his urging and publicly dedicated his baby sister Irene at a mission street meeting.

Weeping May Endure for a Night *Psalm 30:5*

(As Told by Wilfred)

In 1929, at the time of the stock market crash, Dad was earning $18 a week, hardly enough to pay the rent and feed two adults, two teenagers, and two younger girls. The grocer let us charge our purchases. Each payday Mother would send him what she could, but it was never enough; our bill kept escalating.

I saw the smile leave Mother's face. Although she didn't attend church, she had always sung the hymns of her youth. Mother stopped singing. My heart was crushed. I can still see my dear mother worrying over budget figures. The ever increasing debt reached $200! How could we live long enough to pay it?

After eighth grade graduation, I asked for a summer job at the Canadian National Telegraph Company. Even though they were not hiring and I was small at 15, my persistence and earnestness got me the job. Every two weeks I signed over my check, $15 to $20 to my mother. Those four checks that summer helped her smile again; she began to sing again.

That settled it. If that bit of money would bring the song back to Mother, I would continue working for a year. I studied typing and bookkeeping at night school to supplement my meager education. I knew I needed it to be a missionary.

Those first few months were terrible. The 27 other delivery boys were older than I, had greater seniority, and pushed themselves ahead of me to get the telegram when it was my turn. They were a smoking, drinking, carousing, vile-speaking bunch. They entertained themselves by initiating newcomers. Since there were no new employees, they "initiated" me repeatedly. It was horrible. The thugs forced me to the basement. I often wondered why my mother never asked whatever happened to my underclothes. She would see them covered with shoe blacking, pencil shavings, and so on. Another game they played was dismantling my bicycle. There I was, with a limited time to deliver several telegrams, and my bike would be in pieces, or out of sight. Once it was on top of a building.

When they knew I was a "preacher" they did all they could to humiliate me. Once, nine of them ganged up on me, two grabbing each arm and each leg and one opening a bottle of beer. "Let's make the preacher drink," they boasted. As I squirmed they tried to pour it down my throat. Drenched in beer, I stank until I could get my clothes washed.

Sometimes on weekends they would hang around the street-meeting snickering. I would mount my soapbox to testify and there in the crowd I'd see some co-workers. How they would mock on Monday! It was a hellhole, but later I learned what good preparation it would be for the mission field.

I plowed through snow for a distance of up to three miles in minus 25° to 30°F (-30° to -35°C) weather to deliver those telegrams. At times the clerk warned, "This is a death message. Get the signature quickly and make a speedy departure."

None of us wanted to have a lady faint in our arms as she read the telegram—which did happen occasionally. I used to say, "I don't like to deliver death messages. I want to tell people how to live." But I kept on working.

When we were shot at on the mission field; when a revolver was put on our chests while I was preaching the gospel, when we endured awful experiences in that decade of violence in Colombia, I often thought, "I used to suffer things almost this bad just to earn a bit of money in Canada when I was a youth. Why should I complain about difficulties here?"

The Great Depression deepened. No way could I quit my job. One year stretched into five. I knew I needed high school to get to the mission field and I was praying my heart out and seeing my hopes vanish by the day.

But Joy Comes in the Morning   Psalm 30:5

"Mom, here's my check. It's the last one. I've worked five years and now I'm going to Prairie Bible Institute [PBI]. I've heard it's one of the greatest missionary training schools in the world, and it's only eighty miles [128 km] away."

He sold his bike for $12; friends gave him what they could. With $25 he started off for PBI. He knew disciplined missionaries were trained there without luxuries. Tuition plus spartan room, board, and laundry cost $3 per week.

"What's your gratis assignment?" asked roommate Bruce. (Every student worked 10½ hours per week to stretch the fees.)

"I guess they've got some cows out there. I have to pump water for them twice a day. It's not bad. I'm used to working outside." In spite of the 40 degrees below, Wilfred reported to Lem, "It's good exercise and I need that." He wrote glowingly of the school. He delighted in the Bible studies, had fun in the singing class, admired his teachers, appreciated roommate Bruce Wannop, and in all was jubilant about Prairie. The atmosphere contrasted dramatically with that of the telegraph company, and he was progressing toward the mission field. To his mentor, Lem Fowler, he wrote:

Prairie Bible Institute
Three Hills, Alberta
Oct. 16, 1934

My dear brother Lem,

Thank you for your message. I have thanked our heavenly Father every time I have looked at it. I love and reread your letters which mean much to me and imagine I hear you speaking to me. Although I love the Lord, I do not esteem His Word as much as a letter from a human friend. Even in this hallowed place, it's hard to study for love of the Word, rather than as a duty. But keep on praying. I need it as much as ever.

Classes are most blessed. Miss Miller teaches Bible I, three one-hour lessons a week. They aren't easy lessons, either. I spent two-and-a-half hours on the first chapter of Genesis, and when I went to class, I hardly knew anything. She also teaches two periods a week of ancient history. Today we were studying the origin of man and the errors of evolution. I never knew there was so much in the first chapter of Genesis!

I have only one hour a week with the principal, Mr. Maxwell—personal work. That's my favorite class. Then there's Bible atlas, English, spelling—I got 94% on the placement test, and maybe I can take homiletics in place of music theory because of my piano lessons when I was in grade school. I am so grateful that Mom and Dad sacrificed to let me learn piano through third level.

We have a nice room and Bruce is artistic in making it pretty and cozy. We have wonderful food: roast beef on Sunday, salmon cakes today, fruit most meals. It's hard to get used to the new surroundings. The atmosphere is certainly blessed, but I miss the Mission. Please don't think I am complaining; I have no reason for that. Everything is lovely.

"If ye then be risen with Christ
seek those things which are above.
Set your affections on things above,
Not on things on the earth" (Col. 3:1,2).
By God's grace, that is my aim.

Your little brother in our loving Father,
Wilfred

That fall Wilfred publicly dedicated his life to foreign missionary service. He told the Lord he was counting on His help—he would do his part but he was trusting God to help him over the obstacles of poverty, limited education, and lack of church backing.

In Everything Give Thanks   *I Thessalonians 5:18*

A dollar here, a dollar there—money came in to keep Wilf's account clear, but not a cent to spare. Christmas vacation found his pockets empty.

Some students were driving a full car to Calgary. Wilfred prevailed upon them to let him ride in the empty open trunk. Eighty bumpy, cramped, bitterly cold miles away Wilfred was delighted to be with his family and the Mission. He was excited to talk with his sister Liela, his dearest pal. She had married a fine, hard-working, well-salaried older gentleman. They and others gave the student cash gifts, so he was able to finish the year debt-free. Subsequent events would cause Wilfred to remember that trunk ride with deep appreciation.

God Works in All Things for Good   *Romans 8:28*

"'Nightmares', anyone?" The bags of straw weren't for horses, but for students who had vacated their dorms and lined up straw ticks in the classrooms.

Hundreds of visitors poured in to Three Hills on Saturday afternoon. Wilfred was eagerly anticipating that final week of his freshman year—the missionary conference, graduation, and Easter.

The guests occupied the dorm and the students bedded down in the classroom. In the stillness, broken only by snores and loud breathing, footsteps were heard. "Mr. Watson. Is Mr. Watson here?" Wilfred awoke and responded.

"You are wanted on the phone." Throwing on what clothes he could find, Wilfred rushed through the bitterly cold night to the office building, wondering who could be calling him. For six months no one had phoned him. It was his mother in Calgary.

"Wilfred, Liela is in the hospital, very, very sick."

"What's the matter?"

"She had some women's difficulties. The doctor didn't realize she had a cold and gave her ether that loosened the phlegm in her bronchial tubes and lungs. She's choking to death."

"Mother, I'll be there first thing in the morning." Wilfred looked around. The office building was deserted. Nobody would be driving to Calgary tomorrow. All would be coming out to Three Hills. He had to wait for the morning bus.

Half blinded by tears, he fought his way through the snow to the classroom. Feeling his way in the darkness he found his straw tick. Prayer replaced sleep. "Lord, save my sister. Please spare her."

Bundled up with what clothes he had available, Wilf trudged two blocks to town for the 8:00 bus. If stomping around the station had been efficacious, the bus wouldn't have been an hour late. But the snow limited visibility, delaying the run. Impatiently, the brother combined crying out to God and trying, mentally, to push the bus to make it go a little faster.

An eon later, the driver pulled the bus into the Calgary station and Wilf jumped off and raced home. His mother was in the big easy chair, crying. Dad, with his hands deep in his pockets, paced back and forth. Liela had died and the sun had gone out of their sky.

After the funeral, after that casket went down into that deep, dark hole and the grave was filled with chunks of frozen earth and ice and snow, the grieving family returned to their bungalow.

"Dad," began Wilfred. "My sister is in heaven and some day I'm going to go there. I'll see her again, Dad, but you won't."

"Why, Son?"

"Dad, you know why. You've never accepted the Lord Jesus as your Savior."

Wilfred recalled the countless times he had broached the subject. Always his dad would reply, "Am I not a good father? Don't I take good care of your mother?" He *was* a conscientious, hard working, moral man but he still needed Christ like anyone else.

"You know why, Dad. Because only people who have been saved will go to heaven."

Dad Watson knelt beside a chair and cried. Never before had Wilfred seen his strong father cry. And it wasn't because his daughter was in the cemetery. It was because of his sin. "Lord, save me," he pleaded. Turning around, Wilfred saw his mother also kneeling, asking the Lord to save her. Gratitude filled his heart that even on that dark, dark day, both parents had entered the family of God.

Sowing Seeds of Righteousness   *II Corinthians 9:6-10*

The Great Depression continued. Wilfred needed a summer job, but jobs were scarce. He and his roommate had prayed about it and talked it over.

"Wilf, do you want to do farm work?" Some 80% of Alberta was rural in those days.

"I don't know the first thing about it, Bruce."

"Dad needs help on his farm but last year's crop was miserable and he's broke. He needs help, now, but he just doesn't have money. If you would go with me to Scollard [northeast of Three Hills] my folks will give you room and board and love you like a son. Then this fall Dad will put you on his threshing team and you'll earn enough to get back to school."

"Don't do it, Wilf," advised another dormmate. "Bruce is trying to take advantage of you. You can find a better job than that."

"I doubt it. There isn't much other work available. I'm no farm hand but I believe the Lord wants me to work with Bruce's parents."

"What will your mother think? And aren't they looking forward to having your help at the Calgary Gospel Mission?"

"Mother won't like it, and Fred wants me to help at the mission. And Lem will be disappointed. But I feel the Lord has opened this way, and it is not for me to let human desires come before His. Six month's hard work will do me good. I'm beginning to feel the need of a little strenuous exercise and I could learn many valuable lessons."

"Will you be able to do any evangelistic work?"

"Yes, Bruce tells me there are two places where he preached last year and there will be lots of opportunity for service."

After Liela's funeral, Wilfred returned to school. The Wannops came for Bruce, and Wilfred climbed into the car, becoming one of the family.

The city boy had lots to learn on the farm: milking cows twice a day, working with horses, plowing, harrowing, everything!

Sunday afternoons they drove to a one-room schoolhouse where Bruce had preached for several summers. Bruce was gone part of the summer which gave Wilfred his first opportunity for formal preaching—other than giving his testimony on the street corner. How it thrilled him to see people helped and blessed by his messages!

Harvesting in Alberta in 1935 was hard work. The wheat had to be cut while it was still green to hasten the ripening. "Look, Wilfred," instructed Dad Wannop. "The stooks of eight sheaves have to be set up on end so the wheat dries and doesn't sprout. You gotta be careful with this stooking."

"I'll pay you two dollars a day for stooking and three-fifty a day for the threshing."

"Watch those stooks, Wilfred, m' lad. If you don't stand them up properly the wind'll blow them over." And many a stook did get blown over, and Wilfred had to reset it.

Then came threshing! It, too, was hard, hot work. Loading those hay racks was trickier than one might think. If not done right, the rack can be almost loaded, and then one side would slip out. It was hard enough to do it once, but Wilfred often had to do it repeatedly. He appreciated the farmer's patience and the opportunity to learn so much.

Wilfred returned to Prairie with over one hundred dollars! Some of his friends still criticized Mr. Wannop saying he had taken advantage of the city boy. But years later Wilfred looked back on that experience and said, "That was the best investment I ever made. Mr. Wannop was one of my best prayer supporters. He lived to be an old man and until his death he prayed for me daily. When I was in South America he sent me money every six months, or at least every harvest, for years and years. He was a real good friend."

Wilfred continued to room with Bruce for his second and third years and continued to appreciate the life and studies at PBI.

After his second year, he and Bruce with classmate Blair Lytle formed a gospel team. Their pooled resources of $50 bought a Model T Ford, with $10 left to buy a new spare tire and a tank of gas. On the back of the car they painted bold white letters on black, "PREPARE TO MEET THY GOD. AMOS 4:12."

Schoolhouses were available for services. Sleeping quarters were in the car, in the moon light, in hay lofts, and occasionally in kind people's homes. Witnessing took place on the road (car sign), at gas stations, and wherever God gave opportunity. They saw all this as wonderful preparation for missionary service. They met Christians who prayed for them and supported them throughout their missionary careers.

Harvest time, and all hands were needed! Wilfred contracted with Mr. Wannop and two neighboring farmers to stook the sheaves. Before breakfast he would stook one field—unhindered by the harvesters. By early afternoon he'd set up the second field. From four o'clock well into the moonlight he would be working the final field. Day after day he repeated this procedure. He never forgot the kindness of one farmer who sometimes, early in the morning before the grain was dry enough to be cut, would set up a few of the stooks, yet never docked him on the full contract price.

Again it was threshing time! With a good team of horses, Wilf worked like a veteran. The ladies on each farm tried to outdo each other with the victuals, and the smallest of the threshers held his own with the biggest of the eaters!

Back at Prairie, Wilf's leadership qualities and heart for missions gained him the position of South America Prayer Group leader. That and participation in three choirs did not diminish his determination to keep at the head of the class, in spite of his lack of secondary education.

Toward the end of his junior year, funds ran out and Wilf considered quitting. Indebtedness was unthinkable. But Principal Maxwell encouraged him to continue. Another farming opportunity that spring enabled him to pay up. The elderly farmer became a faithful friend and lifetime prayer warrior for Wilfred. He would have kept him for the summer, but Wilf had already committed himself to work with the Canadian Sunday School Mission in the Peace River country in northern Alberta, far beyond the highways.

Ever seeking opportunities to witness, Wilf and his companion, Blair Lytle, sang gospel choruses and hymns on the long train rides to Edmonton and beyond to Spirit River, near the Yukon. They passed out hymnals and had a regular song service.

In describing the last leg of the journey from Peace River to Spirit River, Wilfred wrote to Lem:

> That trip of 65 miles [104 km] was enchanting. The scenery resembles a rich, semitropical country .... We crossed the Peace River on a ferry .... For location, the town of Spirit River is unexcelled. The center of a large wheat-growing area, it is an aggressive little town and would stand against almost any town in Southern Alberta for stores, cars, and *sin*.

At the end of three weeks of evangelistic meetings in a rented circus tent, Wilf wrote, "We estimate the worth of our service in the glory it brings to God." They were thrilled to find a few Christians in town, and rejoiced in the Lord's provision.

Blair returned to Calgary, but Wilf remained, ministering to some who came in from the country. Notable was the Edey family which was later saved and became stalwart Christians. Mr. Edey became a member of the Board of Directors of the Peace River Bible Institute (PRBI). Eventually six of the family studied at that school; one went to Indonesia and another to Africa, both with WEC, the mission which Wilf later represented.

Prior to the tent meetings, teenager Charlotte Dale may have been the only Christian in her whole area. At street meetings in Spirit River she always participated and bravely testified before all the people who knew her. She later graduated from PRBI and went to Africa, also with WEC.

Wilfred had become infected with what he called the "missionary rabies" and even in his student days was "biting" every missionary prospect he met.

Returning to Prairie, a piece of his heart remained in the North Country. It thrilled him to know that a young lady from Prairie had stepped in to fill the gap.

God Supplies All Needs   *Philippians 4:18*

"This looks like a summons, Wilf," joked the student mailman. With some consternation Wilfred arrived at the principal's office. Eight more seniors awaited the pronouncement to be made. Of a class of 54, they were chosen to be the class speakers. "The subject will be 'The Christian Warfare,' " began Mr. Maxwell. "Mr. Watson will introduce the subject. Seven of you will each speak on one part of the armor from Ephesians six, and Mr. Hansen will conclude. You will need to present the first draft of your speech in two weeks. We'll have rehearsals in the new tabernacle so you will be accustomed to speaking in such a large auditorium. If you need any help, see me. Do you have any questions?"

The nine recognized the honor and responsibility of representing their class and the Prairie Bible Institute. They would surely do their best, with God's help.

Returning to his room, Wilfred examined his scanty wardrobe. He looked at his trousers that were kind of decent, and his sport jackets that were acceptable. His second-hand suit used for his summer preaching ministry was shot. Nothing appropriate for graduation! On his knees he pleaded for a suit. "Lord, I'd get up there in a bathing suit if I had to; but, Lord I do need a new suit. I should have one to graduate." His fall threshing jobs had barely paid for expenses. There was no money for a large item. His dad wasn't working; he couldn't write to his folks for help. With whom could he discuss his plight? He had never told people his needs, and now he would tell only his Savior. "Lord, I need a suit!" Simple clothing was appropriate for campus life, and certainly appropriate for his "gratis work." No, he hadn't pumped water for the cows since that first winter. He had been the storekeeper for three years—keeping track of the groceries for the institute family of some five hundred people. He received the weekly supplies off the grocery trucks from Calgary.

A month before graduation Wilfred was praying as he handled those huge cartons. He prayed for his family, for the mission, and for many others. But he was praying also about graduation—the speech that he kept rehearsing in his mind, and for the proper attire. "Lord, I need a suit."

"Is your name Watson?" inquired the truck driver.

"Yes, Sir."

"Down in Calgary somebody gave me this and said he hopes it will fit you," and he threw him a big package. Duty before pleasure, and Wilfred had to stow away all the groceries.

The excited senior trudged through the snow to his dorm. Upon opening the package he saw a handsome three-piece navy blue suit that fit him to a T. His gratitude knew no bounds—to the friend who chose to remain anonymous and to the Lord who had answered his prayer.

Graduation Day! The greatest joy for Wilfred was his family's first visit to Prairie; the greatest disappointment, Lem Fowler's absence. As a traveling salesman he was out of Alberta. From Calgary Wilfred wrote to Lem about the graduation activities, expressing his thanks for the congratulatory telegram Lem had sent him. About his family, he wrote:

> Mother was here ten days and the Lord did great things for her. After the Sunday evening service she testified of God's blessing at the convention saying she was going to live out what the Lord had given her these days. Dad brought Muriel and Irene for a few days and they were greatly revived.

During his senior year, Wilfred had corresponded with mission boards. The first one required high school and Bible School diplomas, to be under age 30, and pledges totaling $50.00 per month. The second said the same, but required pledges of $75.00 per month. Wilfred was 24 and was about to graduate from Bible School, but the other two requirements were hopeless. He had no church connection other than the little city mission. His dad, when working, made about $65.00 per month. The Great Depression continued, and everybody he knew was just scraping by.

Then he read the story of C. T. Studd, founder of the Worldwide Evangelization Crusade (WEC) and began corresponding with Mr. Ruscoe, director of the newly established North American WEC headquarters. Rusiko, as he was affectionately called, was interested in Wilfred since he himself also had left school at age 15 and also had lived with poverty. No monthly pledged support would be required. He checked Wilfred's references and his satisfactory medical exam and advised him of the "seal money" policy: trust the Lord for $250.00 to be sent to the mission, which would be used for his outfit and transportation.

"I may as well return to the Peace River country to do home mission work," thought Wilfred. "That seal money hasn't come in."

Checking his funds, Wilf realized he didn't have enough for the 500 mile (800 km) train trip. Still, he would make his needs known only to God. Should he buy a ticket for as far as his money would take him, and then trust the Lord for the rest? No, God gave him a better plan.

With backpack and suitcase Wilfred started hiking. Two miles out of Calgary, an Edmonton schoolteacher, driving back in the blizzard after Easter vacation, picked him up. As Wilf began praising the Lord for His provision the driver assured Wilf that he, too, was trusting the Lord. They enjoyed blessed fellowship for 200 miles (320 km).

In Edmonton, the Lord again provided, with two good days in the hospitable Cunningham home. Don and Angus Cunningham had been at Prairie with him. Don introduced him to a businessman preparing to drive to Peace River who took Wilf with him.

> I shall never forget his kindness [wrote Wilf]. He bought me the best of meals, and since his business delayed the trip, he arranged lodging for me. I learned some valuable lessons from this experienced Christian.

God reinforced the principles of trusting the specific leading of the Lord and of looking to Him alone for his needs.

Arriving at Spirit River, Wilf was thrilled with the spiritual growth of his host family. Mr. Dale paid him $15 per week for working six long days. Wilfred saw his gospel work as being his Sunday preaching ministry, but God was using him every one of those work hours to mold and teach the Dale family: lessons of praise, lessons of gratitude, lessons of faithfulness, and lessons of setting the "affections on things above." That July he wrote:

> The Peace River country is exceptionally dry this summer, but the Lord has abundantly blessed us with spiritual showers. The hard circumstances cause people to lift their eyes from the transitory things of this life to the eternal.
>
> The crop disappointments make me wonder if the divine Husbandman is disappointed in the fruit that our lives yield Him. My constant prayer is, "Lord, make me a fruit-bearing Christian." And the reply is always the same, "He that abideth in Me and I in him the same bringeth forth much fruit." Commenting on Matthew 5:3, F. B. Meyer said, "It is the drooping (poor in spirit) ears that are heavy with corn; the stems that hold their heads erect are empty and worthless." Lord, help us to be humble and fruitful.
>
> Please pray that God will send a permanent worker to these needy and fruitful districts. One unsaved and supposedly hardhearted man with a large family on relief sends his family to the services. "Watson's religion is the one for us," he told a friend. "If he comes here to work we will feed him." I wish I could stay here, but perhaps someone who cannot take my place in South America will come here.

Late that summer he got a job on a big threshing crew. The threshers saw this little fellow, about 115 pounds, city-slicker, and to boot, a preacher. They anticipated great fun!

> But, [wrote Wilf] it wasn't long before they realized that I could hold my own with the work with anybody on the outfit. I got my team in as fast as anybody else, even though my poor horses were hard to handle.
>
> The first night in that big portable bunk house, I pulled out my Bible and began to read. They thought that was a big joke, but before long they asked if I would read out loud. So I did, and gave them my testimony. There was some mockery but before we were finished two of the worst ones decided to visit the church and hear me preach. One of them accepted the Lord and became a valued friend.

Later, in the British army, the new convert wrote expressing his gratitude to Wilfred for helping him to find the Lord Jesus, his Stay, his Security, and his Help.

Torn between wanting to proceed to South America—but not having the seal money, and the pull of the North, Wilfred returned to Calgary to enlist the help of Bruce Wannop for the winter.

However, in mid-July he had written to Lem, "I have felt all summer that this fall I would be able to get started on my way, and I am still believing that."

The end of October Mr. Ruscoe phoned Wilfred from Toronto. "How much of your seal money do you have?"

"Fifty dollars have been given to me and I've saved fifty from what I've earned."

"Well, you come with what you have. I've received several sums of money for you. We need you here in Toronto."

Ladies at the Calgary Gospel Mission prayed for missionaries, especially for Canadians and for those from Prairie. It was a special privilege for Wilfred to meet with those "Prayer Mothers" one November afternoon. They requested him to bring a photograph, which they placed on the piano. These little old ladies—mostly under 50, but seeming old to Wilf with their funny hats and long skirts—promised to pray for him unitedly as well as individually. At the conclusion of the service they invited him to the front. In the familiar surroundings of his beloved mission, he knelt and an elderly pastor laid hands on him. Not having been ordained, he was especially grateful for that blessing and commissioning service.

Returning years later at furlough times, he always found his picture on the piano and the ladies praying for him. In fact, 48 years later he had the joy of visiting one in a nursing home. "Wilfred," she said, "I'm the last of those ladies who prayed for you. We prayed for you, and we prayed for our children. Three of mine are serving the Lord on the mission field."

The day of departure for Toronto arrived! All of his Calgary friends were at the train station. One of the "Prayer Mothers" came with her trumpet. Some of his friends handed him a sacrificial dollar or two. The air was charged with joyful excitement.

Wilfred reached out to embrace his beloved mother. But instead of adding to his joy, she blurted out, "You're not a good Christian. You're my only boy and we need you."

"Mother, my dear mother. I know I was a bad boy and gave you some nightmares before I was saved. But since then I've tried to redeem those years. I've tried to be obedient, and I've tried to be a good son." "You could be a pastor here at home. But don't go to the mission field. You're leaving us all alone!" Time was up and he almost had to push her away so he could board the train. The heavy-hearted son had his most joyful day turned to sadness. But the Lord had a special balm for him several hours later when he was able to stop off in Regina for a few days with his special friend and mentor those 15 years, Mr. Lem Fowler.

Six good months in WEC headquarters followed. In June of 1939, he was sent to New York to board an ocean liner for Colombia, South America.

In September of that year Canada entered World War II. Suddenly, Mrs. Watson realized that had she held onto her son, he might have been drafted and sent to war. Then she wrote to him, "Wilfred, I'm so glad you're a missionary. Now you don't have to be a soldier."

Chapter II

INITIATION TO THE MISSION FIELD: COLOMBIA, 1939-1942

Content with What You Have   *Philippians 4:11*

"Steerage is down that staircase." Wilfred was traveling third class. Why? Because there was no fourth class! At the bottom of the stairs a policeman tried to stop him. "Civilized people can't go down there. I'm guarding these cutthroats, deportees. I leave with the pilot." "Here's my ticket. I have to go in." Reluctantly the officer admitted him. A quick count indicated 30 double-deck beds occupied by rather scrubby-looking Chinese and Latins. When the ship left dock, Wilfred ventured upstairs, leaving his footlocker, suitcase, and box of books under his assigned bed. For five days he enjoyed the company of the prisoners and his first Spanish lessons!

Buenaventura, (see Glossary) the Pacific Coast seaport, was two mountain-ranges away from Bogotá which is situated high in the third range (see maps starting on page 143). The field leader, Mr. Pat Symes, met the ecstatic newcomer who, gazing at his strange surroundings, felt his heart overflow with gratitude to God for taking him to South America—and to WEC. Even the two-day bus trip over the mountains didn't dampen his spirits. He couldn't talk with the people, but he compensated by distributing gospel literature.

With Stammering Lips and Another Tongue He Speaks   *Isaiah 28:11*

Concentrated Spanish study followed. Eight hours of formal study was followed by a daily errand on the antiquated city busses when a fellow missionary helped him with Spanish. A local carpenter would talk nonstop for two hours while Wilf wondered what it was all about. On Sundays he attended Catholic Church in the morning (he liked the priest's perfect Spanish) and the WEC church in the afternoon. He replaced his English Bible with the Spanish one.

The young WEC church in Bogotá lacked mature workers. To fill a vacancy, Wilfred was asked to superintend the children's Sunday School. With his stumbling Spanish he befriended the children. He enjoyed talking with them one-on-one in their homes. He took a special interest in

Washington Padilla, the small son of a Christian layman. Wilf recalled how Lem Fowler had discipled and mentored him and now he, in turn, had the joy of influencing another lad in the Christian walk. Even as Mr. Fowler had no way of predicting the extent of Wilfred's ministry, so "don Wilfredo" could not have imagined how his little friend would become a prominent evangelical educator and administrator of Ecuador. In an article published a few years before his death, Washington, in describing his theological journey, wrote:

> Another artless soul who had a decisive impact on my theological formation was a humble Canadian missionary who worked in Colombia for some years and then passed to Venezuela, Wilfred Watson. "Don Wilfredo" as we called him, was an excellent teacher and a lover of children. I still remember on my fingers many of his object lessons. They were always simple, designed to teach us some aspect of the gospel or the Christian life. Another of his teaching methods was to have us learn verses or entire chapters of the Bible. The prizes he gave us were books that stimulated our imagination: exploits of the great explorers, conquerors, scientists, missionaries and servants of mankind.
>
> Nor was the teaching of don Wilfredo limited to the Sunday School classroom. Frequently he visited our home. He took some of his older pupils to distribute gospel tracts in the neighborhoods of Bogotá, and he even invited us to accompany him to nearby towns for the same purpose. It is not surprising that at the early age of twelve I felt the call of God to dedicate my life to the preaching of the gospel.

After four months in Bogotá, Wilfred was asked to play the wedding march for his Spanish teacher, a second-generation missionary. (She then joined her husband in his missionary work and the language classes ended.) He was forever grateful to the Lord for those years of piano lessons that his music-loving parents had provided for him during his upper elementary school days when they lived in a company-owned house with a piano.

Sometimes limited comprehension gets missionaries into hot water, even in cold country. And Bogotá is always cold, 8600 feet (2620 m) up in the mountains. Offering tracts is easier than talking to people, but Wilfred attempted both. In a remote area he was invited in to talk, and

"No tiene papá."
(He doesn't have a daddy.)

the lady agreed to host a meeting in her home the following week. Monday afternoon he biked out there and invited some of the neighbors to the meeting. He played his autoharp, sang for them, gave a little message, and invited them back the following week. That time, instead of five, ten showed up. After the service, when the others had left, the hostess offered Wilfred some hot chocolate. As he warmed his hands on the handleless mug, he looked around at the adobe walls and mud floors. The two little rooms boasted not one piece of decent furniture. He had seen only one child in the house. Newness to the language limited subjects he could discuss, but he could ask about the child's father.

"*No tiene papá.*" (He doesn't have a father.) Her next question sent Wilfred hurriedly on his way: "Wouldn't you like to be his father?" Gulping down the scalding chocolate, Wilfred ran out, jumped on his bike and never returned.

Serving the Lord with Gladness   Psalm 100:2

Some important aspects of missionary work are behind the scenes. Prior to his summers on the Alberta farms, Wilfred had considered himself nonmechanical. However, when he saw the WEC press in Bogotá idle for lack of funds to pay the Colombian printer, he began tinkering with it. During four months of language drill, he found typesetting an interesting diversion as well as wonderful language study. Being asked to run it permanently was another story. He hadn't come to Colombia to print and was tempted to consider it second best. But as he submitted the situation to the Lord he came to the conclusion:

> There is no doubt the literature we put out is worth its weight in gold. I believe the Lord will yet enable me to see the full importance of this work if He wants me to stay here.

Four months later he wrote victoriously:

> The Lord is blessing the press and I believe He has given me a service that is indescribably interesting. This work would thrill the heart of any young fellow who loves to see gospel literature going out. We hope to soon send out tracts to all missionaries in Colombia without cost....

The following year he wrote:

> Our hardworking press printed 20,000 tracts last week: some for us but mostly for other societies. In April we finished printing three books (with 156, 25, and 30 pages respectively). Recently we shared a stand with the British & Foreign Bible Society at the major book fair in the government building. They sold $575 worth of Bibles and we sold $60 worth of gospel booklets (mostly five- and ten-cent sales). We are highly pleased and see returns for our labors.

Wilfred continued working in the print shop until the 1942 field conference, when he was released to engage full time in that itinerant evangelistic work in which he exulted.

How Good and How Pleasant to Dwell Together in Unity!   *Psalm 133*

Four hours of beautiful scenery in a bus making hairpin turns, ever downward, ever warmer, under a waterfall, past crosses and shrines marking locations where vehicles had tumbled over the edge—all this fascinated Wilfred in his first venture to the Colombian plains.

Beyond the city of Villavicencio he visited Andres, a lonely Christian who rejoiced to learn truths from God's Word. When the local priest heard of the Bible study, he commanded Andres to attend church on Sunday. If not, his house would be burned, his coffee bushes chopped down and his crops destroyed. Reluctantly Andres complied. He was required to crawl on his hands and knees the length of the church and ask pardon for having become an evangelical. He acquiesced but still as he walked out of the church the congregation grabbed him and beat him almost to death. Perhaps that priest did not know that the blood of the martyrs is the seed of the church.

Wilfred also paid for that trip,—with a six-week bout with malaria when he returned to Bogotá.

Nobody else being available, Wilfred responded to a letter addressed to a Christian magazine by one who had accepted the Lord through reading a gospel tract. A few hours by bus and 15 miles (24 km) by rented horse brought Wilfred to Gachala where he expected to find a big burly blacksmith. Instead, he encountered a fine-featured, curly-headed, dark-skinned lightweight, smaller than himself. When Luis Aguilar realized that Wilf was a missionary he dropped his hammer on the floor and with those sooty arms and hands gave a welcoming bear hug! Graciously he prepared a bed for Wilfred in his own room and escorted him to the best eatery in town, instructing the cook to feed his honored guest. In spite of the debris on the floor, the soiled oilcloth on the table, the poorly washed dishes, the unpleasant noises, and the foul language, Wilf declared the meals to be "just terrific" as he shooed the flies off the food. Luis, a true Christian, rejoiced to meet one other who also knew the Lord.

On Sunday the new companions distributed tracts at the plaza and held a service at the only place they could engage—the local pool hall. An attentive crowd listened as Wilfred used his flannelgraph board to show and tell how Noah and his family were saved in the ark. Luis was thrilled as Wilf explained that Jesus is our ark of safety in whom we can hide, and when the judgment comes on the world, we will be saved.

Wilfred returned a second time—and a third time—even though he was broke and had to hike the final 15 miles (24 km). Luis accompanied him cross country to visit Julio who had been listening in the pool hall and wanted to know more. Julio's large family listened excitedly. Luis had to get back to work, so he left Wilf there to explain more of the gospel.

In his December 1940 letter Wilfred reviewed the previous year of monthly visits to Gachalá:

> With each visit the work goes ahead. At the last visit a man invited me to his beautiful, isolated ranch far up on the mountain. For three days we talked of the Lord—and ate! My Bible studies have never been richer since I left Bible School. Julio was saved through reading a Bible which he bought two years ago and which is his best friend. He has thoroughly and intelligently read it more than once. Eagerly he asked me to explain many things. My heart was shamed and blessed as I talked hour after hour with this hungry, tireless listener. Because he lives what the Bible teaches, he is the avowed enemy of the priest; but he is fearless, true, and spiritual, a delight to me. He wants to be baptized, as does Luis, my beloved blacksmith friend. Others are weak, but earnest. *Pray!*
>
> Our precious hours of biblical conversation were often interrupted by his good wife asking us to the diningroom. I told him that I did nothing but eat and talk. He said, "That's why I brought you here."
>
> The final morning we started with a cup of rich, delicious chocolate, a plate of soup with *two eggs* merrily floating about in it, plus *two fried eggs*, a large corn-cake and several slices of fried platano (cooking banana). A fair breakfast for any man! After a short service, *two more eggs*, another corncake and a large cup of coffee. I

prepared to leave, but the señora (wife) said I had to eat again before leaving. *Horrors!!* A plate of rice, potatoes, etc., large enough to make a starving man recoil! When no one was looking I put a couple of large potatoes in a piece of paper and pretended I had eaten a little. After prayer and the usual words of parting, the woman brought me a packet with *four hard-boiled eggs* and corn cake to take with me and that's not *egg*-zaggerated!

Wilfred and Luis dared to revisit don Julio. When the two slight men had walked a couple of miles they approached a fork in the road. Silently, a huge horseman sat glaring at them. As soon as they were out of earshot, Wilf asked, uneasily, "Who's that?"

"He's the priest's helper. He is a bad man. He has a very bad record."

A bit down the road as they were turning, hopefully out of sight of their antagonist, Wilf glanced back and saw him waving frantically to another rider further down the road. The horsemen galloped toward the prey, who had darted into a house and asked the lady to sell them a cup of coffee.

Pursuing them into the house, the second, who turned out to be the priest's brother, asked, "What are you doing here, Blondie?"

"I'm preaching the gospel."

"The people here don't like the gospel. They don't like that false religion."

Wilfred wasn't able to follow all the rapid harangue, but suddenly he saw the priest's helper dismount and approach menacingly. "What now?" thought Wilf, wondering if this would be his end. But instead of attacking Wilfred, he ripped off his book backpack, remounted, and galloped away.

"Sir, this is robbery. You can't do that here in Colombia," said the daring little foreigner to the priest's brother.

"I don't have your bag." True, but his companion did.

They were allowed to return to Luis's home. The next day Wilfred returned to Bogotá and, with his field leader, reported to the federal police superintendent who called Gachalá with the order: "You return that book bag to that Protestant missionary or I want to know why."

One more trip to Gachalá! This time the whole town knew he had arrived. After host and guest retired for the night they heard an angry crowd yelling, "Down with the Protestants. Kill the heretics." Luis put a big piece of iron against the door, realizing that if the crowd entered, there would be murder. Even though the police arrived and dismissed the crowd, a few crossed the street and continued shouting, "We don't like the Protestants. What are these people doing here?" and, "Let's kill them!" The police kept watch until all was quiet.

The next morning Wilf exited for a brief nature walk but was quickly aware of a crowd of men brandishing machetes. He sprinted back to the house. Luis escorted him out of town. Even though that terminated his visits to Gachalá, it did not end his friendship with the diminutive blacksmith. Luis would one day lead Wilfred to the greatest adventure and blessing of his Christian life.

Chapter III

TEAMING UP FOR MISSIONARY SERVICE IN NORTHERN COLOMBIA AND VENEZUELA: 1942-1954

It Is Not Good That Man Should Be Alone　　　　　　*Genesis 2:18*

Lem Fowler, reading between the lines, gleaned for hints of romantic hope in the letters from his bachelor friend. Early in 1939, Wilf described his life at WEC headquarters in Toronto as the only man with a dozen ladies:

> This place is like a harem. Now I know why they call it bigamy when a man has more than one wife. I think it's pretty "big-o-me" to hold my own against this crowd. The worst of it is, being the only man around the place (when Mr. Gillman is here he is busy in the office) I am "the ladies' aid." I climb ladders, wash windows and do the heavy work when they are housecleaning. I'm not complaining because they do a lot for me. They wash and iron my shirts and always give me a good taste out of the boxes they get from home ....

Lem tried unsuccessfully to identify a "special" member of that "harem." Did he know the WEC principles and practices—that a candidate needed *at least* six months in headquarters before proceeding to the field, and after two years had to be approved at the January field conference before being accepted as a missionary and before marriage could take place? Perhaps there was a pen pal in WEC headquarters.

A full year later, after two years in Colombia, Wilf enjoyed his first vacation. The blacksmith from Gachalá invited Wilfred to accompany him to northern Colombia to visit relatives, offering to pay all expenses.

After visiting Luis's friends and family in Cúcuta, they traveled south a couple of hours to Pamplona, checked in at a local inn (picture a city flophouse of the '30s and downgrade it a few notches) and then ambled over to the Scandinavian Alliance Mission (later known as The Evangelical Alliance Mission, or TEAM), to visit Miss Cora Soderquist—who had visited WEC in Bogotá—and her co worker, Miss Minnie Waage. The delighted hostesses invited the visitors to stay and to preach for them at their Sunday services in that dangerously fanatical area.

Viewing some photos of TEAM co-workers, Wilfred noticed the maid-of-honor in a wedding picture and asked about her. "Cora, would you write to this very attractive bridesmaid and ask her if she would be angry if a young man wrote to her?"

"Sure thing, Wilf," replied Cora, silently wishing that she, herself, might be the object of his attention.

When Elizabeth Lima read Cora's letter, her mind flashed back to a friend who had sympathized with her singleness. She had replied, "Save your sympathy. I'm happy and content in the Lord's place for me." And then how, one evening as she was communing with the Lord, the verse came to her as a bolt out of the blue, "Ye have not because ye ask not." She had said, "Lord, I am happy in my situation, but if You have anyone for me, I want you to lead me." From time to time she had talked to the Lord about the matter but did not become restless.

She recalled, also, the day she had spent with Cora in TEAM headquarters, en route to South America, and the evening walk they had taken. "Elizabeth, do you know what you are doing going out single to the mission field?" challenged the furloughing missionary. "You are sealing your doom to spinsterhood. There are no eligible men on the mission field."

"That's quite all right with me, if that is what the Lord wants," declared the missionary appointee. "I'm going there to serve the Lord. That's my only concern."

So, when Cora's letter came asking if she would object to receiving a letter from a gentleman she hadn't met, she replied, "No, why should I?" She recalled her parents' story of her father taking a name from a list posted in his church in Norway and writing to a young lady in Sweden. Through that, they corresponded, met, and married.

The introductory letter from Bogotá soon arrived. It was promptly answered. In the second letters they exchanged pictures and in his third letter he proposed marriage. The TEAM director personally delivered that letter but had no notion as to its contents nor its source, for the lovers sent their letters to Cora, asking her to read them before repackaging and mailing them.

"Lord," Elizabeth prayed, "It's not for personal reasons that I want to get married. But if I could help him to be a better missionary, I would be glad to say, 'Yes.' "

Now! How were they to get acquainted without the attention of the whole mission? She confided in Harriet and Clara, her co-workers, and in Edna Dade, the bride in the wedding picture. Mr. Dade, the TEAM bookstore manager, remained in the dark. The ladies decided that Wilf should write to Dade asking to visit his store. Of course, the invitation was extended. Using a special gift from the Calgary Gospel Mission Sunday School, Wilfred excitedly traveled in March of 1942 to Maracaibo, Venezuela.

Arriving at the TEAM bookstore, Wilfred was greeted by Dade with the question, "Single or married?" After establishing his bachelorhood, Wilfred was then told, "Sunday I'm going to Los Puertos and there is a new missionary, Clara Carlson, whom I want you to meet." Wilfred knew that Clara was Elizabeth's co-worker, so that was fine with him! Mr. Dade and Wilf ferried across the lake to Los Puertos, where Harriet, Clara, and Elizabeth were stationed. The guests enjoyed the dinner the ladies served and the animated conversation around the table. Mr. Dade never suspected that Wilfred had ever heard of any of the girls before. That afternoon Mr. Dade took the church service in Los Puertos while Harriet drove the others to an outstation where Wilfred would preach and play his 12-base accordion. While Dade supervised, Elizabeth joined Harriet in the front seat; Wilfred sat with Clara in the back. Fine! Just as Dade wanted it! Out of sight, the car stopped and Clara and Elizabeth exchanged places.

The car had problems so Dade, ever trying to connect Clara and Wilfred, suggested he stay over Monday and clean the spark plugs, while he, Dade, returned to Maricaibo by ferry.

Wilfred cleaned spark plugs; the lovers talked. He barely made the last ferry back to Maracaibo. Tuesday the three ladies ferried to Maracaibo for prayer meeting, and there again they saw the visitor. Vacation time was over, and the young swain returned to Bogotá.

The first decade of WEC in Colombia was characterized by spartan sacrifice and suffering. Too many missionaries fell by the wayside; the life was too difficult. Much as Wilfred appreciated WEC and loved his co-workers and his work, the stability of TEAM in both Venezuela and Colombia convinced him not to ask Elizabeth to leave her mission to join WEC. He requested, rather, that she cross the border and together they would minister with TEAM in northern Colombia.

His co-workers were devoted to him and were sorry to see him go; it was wrenching for him to leave them. He remembered with appreciation how they had pooled their little with his insufficient support, and how they had cared for him and paid his expenses when he was gravely ill with malaria. Again Wilfred's heart was touched by their love for him: one of the WEC couples agreed to give her diamond ring to him for Elizabeth.

Much to Elizabeth's delight one April day in 1942, she opened a book that Wilf had printed, bound, and sent to her, *Echoes Poéticos*. Following instructions in his accompanying letter, she cut the spine and found the diamond ring. No postal thief would have looked for a gem in a cheap little book, nor would any mission secretary suspect the significance of a small package coming book mail.

It would be unthinkable to display the ring without prior announcement to her missionary family, so the three romantic co-workers devised a plan. On tiny slips of paper they wrote some words, rolled the papers, and inserted them in numbered medicine capsules. After the missionary prayer meeting, at refreshment time, the capsules were passed out with the instruction to read them according to number. The message came out: "The printshop...spark plugs...flying correspondence...works wonders...Harriet and Clara...in lieu of...Mr. & Mrs. Lima...announce the...engagement of...Elizabeth to... Wilfred Watson." Dade's mouth flew open, "I'm flabbergasted! Hey, I thought it was supposed to be Clara!"

"And who is Wilfred Watson?" asked Mr. Holmberg, the mission director.

"A few months back," reminded Elizabeth, "a visitor at a prayer meeting in your home played the accordion. Remember him?" Yes, then he recalled.

Two big hurdles loomed before them: Wilfred had to be accepted by TEAM and Elizabeth needed a visa to live in Colombia. Wilfred had written to TEAM four years previously and was discouraged by two of their requirements: high school graduation and $50 per month pledged support. He was no closer to getting either.

Elizabeth was granted a visa on American Thanksgiving Day, but with a nearly impossible condition. The visa stipulated that she must marry a Colombian resident (Wilfred) within 30 days of her arrival. The marriage law required them to post bans 20 business days prior to the wedding. A couple of holidays or a delay at the judge's office would frustrate the whole situation.

Wilfred applied to TEAM. He still didn't have a high school diploma, but the mission waived that requirement because of his proficiency in Spanish. But he *did* need $50 monthly support pledged before he could get married. From 1939 to 1942, three and a half years, he had received a total of $350. Six times as much looked impossible!

Elizabeth in Venezuela and Wilfred in Bogotá, Colombia, along with those who loved them and knew the requirements, prayed to the hearing God. In May of 1942 Wilfred had given WEC his six-months notice of leaving. In November, after having made final visits to his preaching points near Bogotá, he farewelled his WEC co-workers and accepted his final assignment with WEC—a book fair in Bucaramanga and Cúcuta. Ties with WEC and the fragile thread of life support were broken. No vis-

ible hope of financial assistance could be detected on the horizon. Having embraced WEC principles of finance, he would not express his need for pledged support, writing only, "There are problems before us, but, 'If God be for us, who can be against us?' No one! Amen!!" The unaffiliated, unsupported missionary was, pending full support, invited to temporarily pastor in La Donjuana, a TEAM country church near the Venezuelan border between the airport city of Cúcuta and Pamplona, where Cora Soderquist taught Spanish to new missionaries. On a previous trip he had ministered in that town of five hundred for a week, accepting the hospitality of a local family. Again he was grateful to church members who provided him three nourishing meals each day while, in the few weeks before Christmas, he:
  became acquainted with the church
  accepted the responsibility of children's meetings at a conference in Pamplona,
  had full responsibility for the planning, preparing and directing of the annual Christmas program,
  taught the adult Sunday School class,
  preached Sunday afternoons,
  conducted services several week nights, either in the church or out in the country, and
  visited in the homes of his parishioners.

In his "spare time" he needed to enlarge, make habitable, and furnish the two-room parsonage to prepare it for his bride. And yet, being the only English speaker in the entire area, he found time to run down the hill half a block from his church to meet the unscheduled busses passing from Cúcuta to Pamplona. He had heard that an American couple would be coming that way en route to TEAM language school. And one day he saw them! Brand new missionaries, Bob and Wilda Savage, exuberantly jumped off the bus and greeted Wilf as though he had been a long-lost brother! During a quick tour of the church and parsonage they barely got acquainted, and it was time to reboard the bus.
At the Pamplona language school, Cora and her students were praying for that lovelorn missionary who wanted to get married but needed $50 per month. "Why doesn't he have support!?" exclaimed Bob.
"Oh, he belonged to one of those faith missions that send their missionaries out with nothing. And now he wants to marry one of our missionaries and he needs full support pledged."

Post haste a letter went to his dad, Dr. H. H. Savage, pastor of a great evangelical church, The First Baptist Church of Pontiac, Michigan. "Dad," wrote Bob, "You want to support missionaries. Here's one who's preaching, he knows the language, he wants to get married, and needs $50.00 a month." So a class of career ladies in First Baptist pledged his full support, retroactive to November, when he first went to La Donjuana.

"So," says Wilfred, "we were able to get married and live happily ever after. Well, almost. We'll tell you the rest later."

Through friends, contact was made with the judge in the county seat who was willing to facilitate the wedding plans. Colombian law recognized marriages performed by Roman Catholic priests, but other marriages could only be legalized by a judge. It was common for the judges to use delaying tactics so as to encourage ecclesiastically-approved marriages. But this judge was happy to marry a Protestant couple who had never been baptized as Catholics.

A month before the Big Day, Elizabeth left Maricaibo, Colombia–bound. Due to a missed train connection to Cúcuta she was stranded at the border in a small village which boasted a "Paradise Inn." She was shown to a bedroom furnished with four pairs of sawhorses, each holding three long planks and a straw mat. Exhausted by the work and activity of packing and moving she wrapped herself in her raincoat and lay down that late afternoon, sleeping soundly until the next morning. What was her surprise when, upon awakening, she looked around and beheld the other three beds occupied by men!

Meanwhile, Wilfred—smitten not only by love but also by malaria—accompanied by Cora, was awaiting his bride in the Cúcuta train station. Failing to find her, they returned to their accommodations to meet the same train the next day.

But Elizabeth, inspired by her three sleeping roommates, caught the early train. Arriving in Cúcuta with no one to meet her, she hailed a taxi to the church where she encountered a stuttering cobbler. He directed her to follow Wilf to the plaza.

Happily reunited, they proceeded to the hotel where they found Cora praying for Elizabeth's safe arrival. The threesome boarded the bus for La Donjuana, changing busses there to detour to post bans with the judge. Back to La Donjuana, and Wilf was sent to bed. Properly chaperoned by Cora, Elizabeth visited the ailing Wilf. Cora made a discreet exit. After a few minutes Elizabeth went out to Cupid Cora who inquired, "Did you kiss him?"

"Uh-uh," muttered the bashful belle, shaking her head.
"Give him a kiss," encouraged the cupid.

Two Are Better Than One　　　　　　　　　　　　*Ecclesiastes 4:9*

The Saturday before the Tuesday wedding 14 guests, 12 from TEAM and 2 from WEC "invaded" that insignificant rest-stop village. All being missionaries, they gladly accepted the accommodations available. Excitement and joy filled the church that Sunday as the visiting missionaries joined the congregation in a baptismal service, baby dedication, and communion. They participated in the music—both vocal and instrumental—and the preaching.

Tuesday morning, February 16, 1943 the bridal couple visited the judge for the third and final time. They and their attendants were overwhelmed by the thoughtful preparations made to facilitate this civil wedding. Rows of chairs were set up for them and for the society folk who wanted to witness the "extraordinary wedding of the two foreigners from the evangelical church in La Donjuana." The judge presented the bride with a bouquet of white roses and shasta daisies. He, his secretary, a newspaper reporter, and another leading citizen accompanied the bridal party to La Donjuana.

The chapel was decorated with pink and white crepe paper streamers, an impressive green archway made of palm branches, white wedding bells, and an abundance of flowers. Wilda Savage played a piano prelude and the wedding march. The bride, dressed in an exquisite gown made by her mother and sister in Oakland, California, was the admired center of attraction. Mr. Christiansen, 35 years a missionary and TEAM field director, honored the couple by performing the ceremony.

Enthusiastic and loving church members served a delicious chicken dinner. A second reception was celebrated in Pamplona with the missionaries.

Wilfred's gratitude knew no bounds for his first wedding gift: $50 monthly support, retroactive to November, from Pontiac, Michigan. With it he bought a pair of fully-equipped horses. Other gifts included a sturdy table with six matching chairs from the La Donjuana congregation; three mahogany chairs with wicker bottoms from a neighboring church; a rocking chair, native blanket, bed spread, table cloth, center table, and gas lamp from fellow missionaries; and money from home with which they bought a bed, gasoline iron, kitchen cabinets, and other furniture. Their

United for Christ

first joint prayer letter detailed their passion for serving their Lord. They wrote:

> The following day we returned to La Donjuana for our "honeymoon," and conducted a three-day series of special meetings. We have covered miles and miles of mountain trails on horseback visiting the homes of people who love us and whom we love and seek to win for God.
>
> Since then we have kept busy with seven regular meetings a week—between us—and usually half as many more cottage meetings, visitation, studying for a week's Bible teaching and upcoming language exams, arranging our little four-room house, and supervising the enlargement of the chapel. Pray for the implementation of an evangelical day school for about 35 children after the construction is completed.

In April, the little church was filled for another wedding using part of the incomplete addition. Wilfred rejoiced to preach the gospel to the many curious people who dared to enter or who clustered around the open doors and windows.

Later that month the Watsons were thrilled that 16 of their church members took time out to accompany them to another town for a one-week seminar where the newlyweds participated in the instruction.

Holy Week services in their chapel were well attended. Although it rained all Saturday night and Sunday morning, over 100 attended the Sunday School. During the morning worship service the Catholics' band blared and skyrockets exploded celebrating the finding of "The Living Christ" (a new image). Wrote Wilfred, "Some of the rockets fell on the tin roof of our church as we were rejoicing over the living Christ who lives in our hearts."

In their few years at La Donjuana the Watsons rejoiced in sending five young people to Bible School. Pablo Rodriguez had been lovingly serving the Lord prior to Wilfred's arrival. In him they discerned a chosen vessel for the Lord's service and encouraged him to apply to Bible Institute in spite of lack of funds. Reminiscent of his own trek to PBI nine years previously, Wilfred mentioned Pablo in a letter to Prairie friends. Great was Pablo's excitement and joy when told that money for his expenses had come through the TEAM headquarters from far away PBI. He could hardly believe that someone that far away would be moved to help him. Immediately he called two of his friends to his room to have a thanks and praise meeting. Wilfred rejoiced to see this attitude of gratitude reproduced in his protégé.

Another great joy to them (and bane to the local priest) was the establishment of an evangelical day school with 45 children taught by an experienced teacher and a local señorita who was being trained on the job. The joys of ministering and seeing spiritual growth in the congregation were mixed with problems. Baptismal classes would be progressing well when it would be revealed that *Fulano*, (so-and-so) who had accepted the Lord and was rejoicing, and growing, and leading his family to Jesus Christ, was not married to his "wife." The Watsons would immediately encourage him to formalize the relationship that had been intact for 25 years. But no, they couldn't get married. "I was married 30 years ago and my wife left me" (we won't ask why) "and lives with another man. They have a lot of children. I haven't seen her since she left, but she's still alive so I can't marry the mother of my children." Wilfred struggled with the Colombian law which did not allow divorce, permitting innumerable similar situations.

Toward the end of the second year of their pastorate, the Watsons were thrilled to have an assistant pastor. Their activities greatly increased. They hoped to leave the work with him while they pioneered another area or left for furlough. Sadly, three months later it was discovered that he had had immoral relations immediately prior to taking this position. To maintain the purity of the work they had to dismiss him, even as they had to refuse baptism, membership, and the Lord's Supper to believers who were living together without legal marriage.

Preparing for his third Christmas program at La Donjuana was much easier for Wilfred than the first one, now with Elizabeth at his side. The children were on the platform when word came that her father was critically ill in Oakland, California.

Airline reservations were unavailable for civilians. (World War II was still raging and Colombia had joined the allies.) On December 26, 1944 Wilfred reluctantly took his bride of two years to the airport in Cúcuta with only uncertain "stand-by" passage obtainable. With no certain itinerary, she boarded a plane to the Caribbean costal city of Barranquilla. Another plane took her to Mexico City and a third to Los Angeles. While waiting to continue north to the San Francisco-Oakland area, she visited her alma mater, BIOLA. A student from her home church joined her in chapel and told her that her daddy had died the day before. Although she didn't get home to see him alive, she did arrive for the funeral.

Back in La Donjuana, Wilfred recalled how, when he first proposed to her by correspondence, Elizabeth had asked him to write to her father, which he did. The godly Norwegian replied encouragingly. That was the only communication Wilfred ever received from his father-in-law. "I missed a lot in not knowing him," thought Wilfred in those lonely days. "But I'm so grateful to him for giving me his lovely daughter to be my wife."

Whoever Loses His Life for My Sake, Shall Find It Matthew 10:39

"Last night they came and killed our cow and chopped down our coffee bushes and burned our home. We don't have anything left."

"Franco, I'm sorry. It's because we came and preached the gospel to you. If we had left you alone, you'd still be up on top of that mountain in Aspasica living without any difficulty."

"No, Brother, don't say that. We still have Jesus Christ in our hearts, and they can't take that away from us."

Sr. Marcos Franco, his wife Rosa, and their eight children had accepted the wise words of Jesus:

> Whosoever will come after me, let him deny himself, and take up his cross, and follow me. For whosoever will save his life shall lose it; but whosoever shall lose his life for my sake and the gospel's, the same shall save it. For what shall it profit a man, if he shall gain the whole world, and lose his own soul? Mark 8:34-36.

The illiterate farmer of the lofty crags of the Andes had, one day several years previously, descended to Ocaña on business. Passing a crude one-room shoe factory, he entered and purchased a pair of *alpargates* (simple canvas sandals with leather soles) for special occasions in town. The shoemaker, a deacon in the church the Watsons pastored after their furlough, wrapped them in scrap paper, Franco tossed them into his string bag with matches, sugar, salt, and items from the hardware store. His business completed, he began the 20-mile climb to Aspasica, mulling over his schemes and intrigues. Cash was important for liquor; avoiding work, equally important.

Part way home he stopped for a meal and a rest with Efigenia, the mother of several of his children. The next morning, after the inevitable argument over money—rather, the lack of it—Franco stomped out of her hovel and proceeded to his mountaintop farm. The walk was long and he had plenty of time to reflect on his recently improved economic situation. The farm was progressing. He had been able to build a house as good as any of his neighbors'—mud brick with a thatched roof. He thought of his small son, Santander, one of Rosa's children, who had been born with a club foot, twisted so that, should he ever walk, it would have to be on the top of the foot rather than on the sole. He recalled how he had suggested that the foot be broken and twisted to the natural position, and his agreement with Rosa to present the baby to "Christ the King"—the most venerated image in those parts. He chuckled as he thought of Rosa's nephew who had come prior to their pilgrimage with a Bible and said they should pray for Santander. Much to Franco's surprise, the foot had straightened out. Strange things do happen!

As he arrived at his farm, hungry and tired, his children scattered. After eating the plate of yucca stew which Rosa served him, he grabbed a package from his string bag. Removing the outer wrapper—it would be useful for kindling—he examined the *alpargates*. In one he noticed a paper—a tiny four-page booklet. Sometimes he wished he could read. After supper he would have one of his children read it to him. Proud of his great accomplishment, the son read from the paper:

FOUR THINGS GOD Wants YOU to KNOW
1. You NEED to be Saved. All have sinned and come short of the glory of God (Romans 3:23).
2. You CANNOT Save Yourself. Not by works of righteousness that we have done, but according to His mercy He saved us (Titus 3:5).
3. Jesus has ALREADY PROVIDED for Your Salvation. For Christ also hath once suffered for sins, the just for the unjust, that He might bring us to God (I Peter 3:18).
4. Jesus Will Enable You to OVERCOME Temptation. If any man be in Christ, he is a new creature: old things are passed away...all things are new (II Corinthians 5:17).

YOUR PART: Repent—(turn from your sins). Except ye repent ye shall all likewise perish (Luke 13:3).
Believe—Believe on the Lord Jesus Christ, and thou shalt be saved... (Acts 16:31).
Confess Your Sins to Jesus—For there is one God, and one mediator between God and man, the man Christ Jesus (I Timothy 2:5).
Confess Jesus Before Men—If thou shalt confess with thy mouth the Lord Jesus, and shalt believe in thine heart that God hath raised Him from the dead, thou shalt be saved (Romans 10:9).

Franco listened with his heart. He had the children read it to him repeatedly. God, who hates sin loved this violent, immoral man and sent a peddler, Elias Rico (Elijah Rich) to this isolated farm. As was his custom in every home he entered, Rico displayed his merchandise, checked on the health of the household, offered medicines, even giving injections—no doctor visited those parts—and then in his cordial way, in spite of a speech defect, shared his greatest riches—the gospel of Jesus Christ. Franco's heart was prepared. In answer to Sr. Rico's question, "Do you believe, Franco, in what the Bible says?" he was ready to reply, "I believe, because I see that my religion never could solve my problems." He asked the Lord Jesus Christ to come into his heart. He was saved!

Next time Franco traveled to Ocaña he revisited the shoemaker. "Sir," he said, "Do you have any more papers like this? Since my son read this to me, I am a different man. My wife says she has a new husband because I don't beat up on her like I used to. My children aren't afraid of me any more. I used to kick them and beat them, and now they want to be with me. Even my dog—my dog always used to stay out of kicking distance because he knew that if he got near my shoe, I'd kick him. Even he knows I'm different. Have you any more papers that can do that to a man?"

The shoemaker, now an elder in Watson's church, bubbled over with joy at hearing the sincere testimony of how God had used that simple tract that he had tucked into the shoe.

"Of course!" He greeted his new brother with a Colombian handshake and bear-hug and gave him several more tracts. He took him to the street and pointed. "Go to that Evangelical Church. There's a foreign couple that will sell you a book for twenty-five cents. It's better than all the tracts put together. It's the Word of God, the New Testament."

Elizabeth responded to his knock on the door and invited him in. He thrilled her with his report of a changed life.

He bought the New Testament and devotedly carried it in his breast pocket. At every opportunity he solicited the aid of any who could read. Books were so scarce that even children who had been in school for two or three years had never handled one. To learn the assignments, they copied from the board. It was an exciting privilege for a child to be able to read the book. Franco listened and remembered and obeyed.

Months later, on November 29, 1946, fellow missionary Elvira (Ivy) Dahlstrom noted in her diary, "Man from Aspasica accepted the Lord. Was so happy I could hardly eat." She later recalled how this *campesino* (country man) had knocked at her school door as she was closing up, wanting an explanation of salvation. He told her about the paper found in his *alpagartes* and about his son reading it to him. For an hour they stood in the open doorway discussing salvation. With her guidance he prayed to accept Jesus as his Savior. He surprised her with his intelligent grasp of the Christian life.

"A man from Aspasica," he told her, "is in jail here in Ocaña. He fears, if he returns home, I'll kill him. I will go to the jail and let him know he need not be afraid any more. I am a Christian now." After a moment of reflection he continued, "I have two families. Which woman should I marry?" The decision was to marry the first one, Rosa.

And, "Doesn't the Bible say something about tithing? Show me where." After reading Malachi 3:10 the man with only canvas shoes, with two families to support (and he did support both to the best of his ability), handed her the full tithe from his coffee sale for the day.

Two weeks later he again visited Ocaña and Wilfred was there. (Major activity at that time was supervising the building of a launch 50 miles away and he had moved closer to the Magdalena River.) The two men were delighted to meet. Franco said, "Brother Wilfredo, I want you to come and dedicate us and our home to the Lord Jesus. We belong to Him and we'd like to have a church."

The Angel of the Lord Encamps Round About Them
That Fear Him....   *Psalm 34:7*

Wilfred, Elvira Dahlstrom, Elias Rico, and four others agreed to visit Franco in a few weeks—on Thursday, December 26th, 1946. Early that morning the seven boarded the north-bound jalopy. After about ten miles they were glad to disembark where Franco was awaiting them with a mule. Miss Dahlstrom mounted the *bestia* while the others hiked about eight miles up the mountain on a narrow ledge—a path barely wide enough for a donkey with two fat bags of coffee strapped over his back, a rock wall to the left, a precipice to the right.

After trudging along for hours, the weary footdraggers suddenly sprang to life. From a dugout cave in the rock, a gang of drunks waved a banner with the virgin's picture on it. They screamed, "Down with the Protestants! Kill the heretics! Long live the Virgin and the Roman Catholic Church!" The temptation to retreat was checked by Franco's encouragement: "Let's keep going. They're drunk. They won't do anything." Cautiously the believers continued upward.

Coming upon a mountain brook, Wilfred pulled up his white trouser legs and gingerly crossed on the stones. Another half hour and they rounded a curve and rejoiced in Franco's glad shout, "There's my home on the corner."

Eagerly anticipating refreshment and rest, Wilfred plunged forward with Miss Dahlstsrom behind him. Gathering around the newly constructed farm house were dozens of people. Wilfred's thoughts, "Great! all these people have come here for a meeting!" were interrupted by Miss Dahlstrom's scream. Looking closer he realized the crowd was armed: revolvers, shot guns, rifles, *machetes* (long knives), stones, and the leader carrying an image. Elvira tore out of there like a streak while Wilfred called, "Elvira! Stay with the group." Exhausted and confused, she obeyed as the rest of their party caught up and the crude crowd of campesinos converged upon them.

The mayor of Aspasica approached Wilfred menacingly, "We don't like the Reds!"

"Good! We don't like them either."

"Well," continued the mayor, "we don't like the Adventists."

"I don't know any of them."

"We don't like you and you better get out of here fast!"

"Sir, we were invited here and we didn't realize we would be a problem to anybody. We'll be glad to go." With an eye on the weapons and the hostile neighbors, the missionary was eager to accomodate. "We don't want to hurt anybody and we're sorry if we have caused any inconvenience."

Pandemonium broke out as the *machetes* began to swing, slashing the men, threatening to cut off Miss Dahlstrom's legs. Her treasured watch was yanked off her arm. Now the up-hill stragglers were leading the pack! Running down that steep mountain trail would have been disastrous, but they set records for speed-walking—and praying—some in Spanish, some in English. In minutes they reached the brook. No bothering with trouser legs this time! What use when they were already splattered with blood?

Wilfred, bringing up the rear, glanced toward the source of the stream. He saw a brute of a fellow, fully twice his size, shirt hanging out over his pants, trouser legs rolled up to the knees, chest covered with grizzly grey beard with two yellow streaks where the tobacco juice had flowed for years from the corners of his mouth. Overcome with fear, separated from the forerunners who had reached the drinking joint, Wilf suddenly understood why the drunks had spared them: they knew what was on ahead and had stayed there to trap the heretics.

The strategy crystallized: "As soon as we get to that drinking joint," thought Wilf, "with one crowd pursuing us and another to block us, they're going to make hamburger of us." His attention was drawn to the giant. Silently he questioned, "Who are you? Where did you come from?"

44   *Teaming up for Missionary Service:*

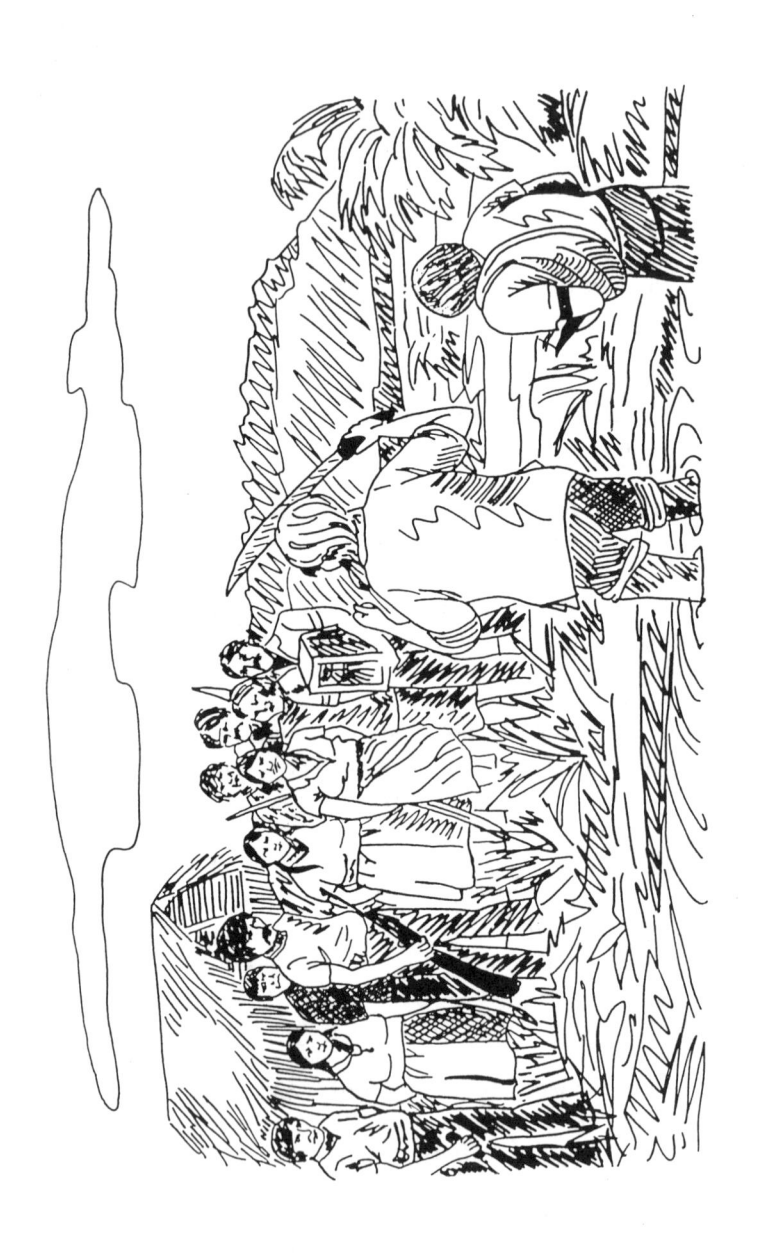

"These people have a right to live!"

As if we don't have enough problems, now ...." Obviously, Wilfred was the target. Any second the giant would step up and slice his victim in two. Step up he did—right behind Wilfred with that menacing machete raised and his left fist clenched. Facing the pursuers and swearing by his own name, he roared, "My name is Gonzalez. I'm a conservative and a good Catholic. But these people have a right to live. I'll kill the first one of you that enters this water!" Having seen the priest serve free liquor and urge his followers to "kill the heretics," this well-known political leader had run ahead and hid in the bushes by the only road from that mountain top. Stunned, the mayor with his gun and all that crowd dared not step into the water.

Franco had been chased to his home; his visitors had gathered at the drinking joint. The drunks were awaiting word from the mayor to proceed with the executions. Frustrated, they screamed, "Where's the mayor? What's happened? Aren't we going to kill them?" Drunk as they were, they realized: no sanction, no massacre. And the mayor was detained beyond the brook.

La Playa citizens had offered police protection earlier. Amazed to see the party return alive, fear kept them from extending hospitality or tending to the knife wounds. Their mayor provided safety in his city hall; but the wounds weren't dressed until the next day, when they returned to Ocaña. "The angel of the Lord encampe[d] round about them that fear[ed] him, and delivere[d] them" (Psalm 34:7).

Even though the missionaries could not return, Franco was allowed to continue living on his farm, but the threats were ominous. Later he had to reestablish his family near the Magdalena River. It was a few years later that, after being officially warned to abandon his religion, his house was burned down trapping him and his family within. Miraculously they escaped from the flaming house and from their pursuers. Destitute of worldly belongings, they made their way to the missionaries as recorded previously.

Don Marcos Franco never learned to read, but he brought his double family and innumerable others to Jesus Christ. Before he went home to glory in 1970, his son and biographer, Jorge Castilla Franco, became a dedicated and effective preacher. Three daughters married preachers. Others of his family also remain faithful servants of the Lord and diligent church members.

I Will Make You Fishers of Men   Matthew 4:19

Riverboat work on the lower Magdalena River challenged the Watsons when they returned from their first furlough in January, 1946 with five-month-old Eric. Their first home that year in the city of Ocaña had a pleasant climate and an established church but was 50 rugged miles from the port. After a few months the Watsons relocated in El Carmen, 20 miles closer to La Gloria, the port town. It was still too far, as Wilfred would spend two or three weeks with the launch and then be with his wife and baby for seven to ten days.

In earlier days, La Gloria had been a tourist attraction where docking cruisers encouraged a thriving business. Due to a shift in the river, an extensive sandbank had built up preventing the docking of coffee boats. Consequently, the frame "Grand Hotel" had been abandoned and had deteriorated.

The proprietor, sympathetic to the gospel as well as to recuperating some of his losses from the hotel, agreed to rent it very reasonably to the mission. The diningroom served for a chapel, two adjoining rooms for living quarters, and two rooms on the second floor for bedrooms.

After renovating and furnishing the chapel, the Watsons began inviting townsfolk to a Sunday evening service. Six adults and 20 children ventured in. Wilfred played his accordion and Elizabeth a small pump organ. He prayed, read scripture, and was about to preach when a drunken policeman entered with eyes flashing. Oaths, accusations, and threats poured out of his mouth. The visitors disappeared through windows and doors leaving the three foreigners in their places. With a revolver inches from the preacher's heart, the inebriate was excitedly shouting, "I am a Catholic and a member of the police force and I'm ready to die for Catholicism. I'm going to put an end to this Protestant heresy right away." This time the protecting "angel" was the police sergeant who succeeded in calming the cop.

However, the drunk did return later that night and fired into the Watson's bedroom, through the plank walls. Praise God, none of the shells hit their intended target.

A few weeks later Wilfred was listening to the Colombian National Anthem on a record with the intention of learning to play it on his accordion. The mayor's secretary entered and announced: "You can't play that here. Give me that record," and confiscated it.

Northern Colombia and Venezuela, 1942-1954 47

For over a year Wilfred and a co-worker studied materials and prices, negotiated, and supervised the construction of the launch, *El Anunciador* (The Announcer). Using $6000 designated for a boat, they built one valued at $10,000. The local priest energetically cursed the gospel launch prophesying that it would sink the day it was floated.

That day arrived and Wilf started the motor which shortly sputtered and stopped. Much as they cranked it, worked with it, and *prayed*, that boat just drifted down river. The strong current was drawing it toward a huge docked barge. Panicking, Wilf rushed to the rear and extended his short arm to hold it away from the barge. An unseen angel protected him and the launch from being sucked under the barge. At that moment an agile quick-thinker jumped off the front with a rope which he tied to a mooring post, stopping the launch just as it was touching that great barge. Satan's plan was defeated and the launch was used successfully for over three years with blessed results.

Persecuted for Righteousness Sake   Matthew 5:11,12

April 9, 1948! A never-to-be-forgotten day in Colombia's history! Volumes have chronicled that infamous day. Every encyclopedia mentions it. "Conservative" means pro-Roman Catholic control; "Liberal," anti-church control and leaning toward communism. The Liberal mayor of Bogotá, Jorge Eliezar Gaitán, the popular candidate for the presidency, was gunned down on the steps of the capitol building. The crowd apprehended the assassin and pounded his brains out on the pavement before any investigation could identify his cohorts. The country went berserk. The city of Bogotá was demolished. Government troops made war on any town that had voted "Liberal." The Liberals murdered priests and other Conservatives. Within hours, the country was in an uproar—initiating the "Decade of Violence."

News of the revolution reached the Watsons at noon of that fateful day in the river town of El Banco. They barely started home when the propeller broke. Wilf managed to remove the offending part and tote it back to El Banco. The town was wild! Nobody was on the job! Amazingly, someone did lend him another prop which Wilf was able to install before the launch became part of the riot. Docking it as usual with the oil company, they gratefully accepted a ride home from an American oilman. Fear, hatred, and violence reigned from capital city (Bogotá) to every hamlet (La Gloria). The landlord was awaiting them at the hotel. "Don't tell anybody, but I've hidden some rifles in your part of the house. People will never suspect you of doing anything like that, so they won't find them."

Not wanting a part in any suicidal intrigue the tenants hastily gathered a few basic items and returned to the launch for refuge. Those were days of prayer stimulated by radio reports.

Wilfred had frequently visited the liberal town of Rio Negro and had been well received. It was no surprise to hear that the people had had an altercation with their two priests. Upon hearing that their hero Gaitán had been assassinated, they rushed to the clergy and demanded mourning bells be tolled. Instead, the two chose to peel a joyous melody celebrating the death of their enemy. The town rose up in arms. The priests hid in the church and shot at the crowds. The people forced them out and shot one and almost decapitated the other. The two escaped and also found refuge in the oil camp in La Gloria where they received care in the hospital.

An army lieutenant (Conservative) approached Wilfred and demanded, "I need your launch to transport thirty soldiers to Rio Negro. We'll kill those rebels."

"Sir, this is a gospel launch. We do not involve ourselves with politics. I have enough enemies without looking for more."

Commandeering the boat, the officer boarded with 30 fully equipped soldiers. Reluctantly, Wilfred conceded to stay with the launch which sank dangerously deeper than ever before. Surprisingly, it made it to Rio Negro. The townsfolk sighted the gospel launch and as one man they ran to the river bank yelling, "*El Anunciador! El Anunciador!*" anticipating news of the revolution and a visit from their preacher-friend.

"Try to calm the people a bit," the lieutenant charged Wilfred when he requested permission to conduct a gospel meeting. Using the loud speaker the missionary led singing, preached, and sold Scriptures.

To the horror of Wilfred and the crowd, those soldiers jumped off the gospel launch, set up their machine guns, and fired at random. Heavyhearted and feeling like a traitor to his friends, Wilfred, with permission from the lieutenant, turned the launch around and motored back to La Gloria.

Rather than return to the rifle-infested hotel the three Watsons found refuge with the oil company. Months passed and the violence intensified. TEAM leaders eventually urged the foreign missionaries to gather in the city of Cúcuta. Wilfred left a young Colombian couple in charge of the launch, authorizing them to occupy the hotel or the launch, whichever they felt best.

The only missionary unable to reach Cúcuta was Cora Soderquist (Watsons' cupid) who, with one of Marco Franco's daughters, was residing in El Carmen. This out-of-the-way town, recently vacated by the Watsons, was emphatically liberal, drawing the ire of the government troops, who entered the town plundering, raping, and massacring indiscriminately. As fellow TEAM missionaries, Elof and Isabel Anderson wrote in their book *Hacaritama* (p. 109):

> In all of Colombia no town is to suffer more. Our missionary ladies are requisitioned to cook for the army. Request to leave town is denied. No one in the outside world is to know of the rape of El Carmen....Food is very scarce.

Cora and Alicia Franco were permitted to search for food. With tensions mounting they hit upon a plan. One noon, with shopping bags on their arms, they ambled from store to store, apparently searching for food, always making their way east toward the mountains. Police were everywhere patrolling but no one questioned them. With hearts beating hard and praying, but outwardly calm, the two left the town and began the 30 to 40 mile (48-64 km) marathon across rough roads over the mountain to Ocaña, resting at night in a liberal town; stopping again at Alicia's home where she remained. Andersons (p. 110) continue:

> Back in town the holocaust reaches a climax, the "coup de grace." The vandals set fire to El Carmen, leaving the city a smoldering ruins.

The missionaries were praying and working. They notified the American consul. They informed reporters who publicized the plight of the two ladies. And "the angel of the Lord encampe[d] around them that fear[ed] Him and delivere[d] them" (Psalm 34:7).

The following day, Thursday, November 25th, 1948, Cora flew from Ocaña to Cúcuta, arriving, like Peter in Acts 12, where foreign missionaries and Colombian Christian refugees were crowded together behind locked doors praying for themselves, for their country, and especially for Cora and Alicia. All those months the benevolence of the American oil company in Cúcuta had been magnanimous, supplying the mission household with food, blankets and so much more. For that day they had supplied turkeys with all the trimmings. The crowd had just been seated and had bowed heads for prayer when a knock was heard. The door was opened and in limped Cora. What a memorable Thanksgiving Day!

As the violence continued, missionary families left Colombia. Illness, furloughs, and transfers to other countries left the Watsons and several single ladies "manning" the TEAM field in Colombia. Wilfred was assigned to pastor the mother church in Cúcuta. Two co-workers, Minnie Waage and Edith Platt, had taken refuge there and were eager to return to the liberal town of Salazar, where they had been conducting a teacher training institute.

The Conservatives of the area vividly remembered election days in the previous decade when armed Liberals had prevented them from going to the polls. Bob Savage's son, Stephen, described the situation in *Rejoicing in Christ*, (p. 11) his biography of his dad:

> The conservatives in Colombia were the ones who supported the Roman Catholic Church without question, exclusively.

The Liberals, in power from 1930 to 1946, were more concerned with the welfare of the people, were greatly influenced by communism, and limited the power of the Catholic church.

> Salazar, [wrote the Andersons, p.104] this Liberal showpiece, appears on top of the Conservative black list, doomed, destined for destruction, to be raped, humiliated, vanquished! For years the Conservatives of the surrounding hills...have been preparing for this assault, savoring the thought of revenge and retaliation.

The two ladies, eager to ascertain whether any of their possessions remained in the deserted house, sought Wilf's aid to return and, as pastor, he presented the matter to his two elders. One, a shoemaker, deceived by the communist propaganda, and seeing the corruption of the church-state, believed communism would lift the poverty-stricken nation, and voted Liberal. The other elder, Teófilo Mesa, a mechanic and Conservative, had been one of those rare ardent Catholics who was offended by what his church was doing to the Protestants.

> He became a friend of Dad's, [wrote Stephen Savage, p. 11] and accepted Dad's invitation to follow Christ, and emerged as one of the pillars of the evangelical church. His voice always carried authority, and over the years of violence in Colombia, especially in the terrible decade from 1948-1958, he often stepped into similar situations and saved fellow evangelicals from mob violence.

With only the two parties, citizens felt constrained to affiliate with one or the other. Together the pastor and his elders devised a plan to pass the road blocks that the Conservatives had erected from Cúcuta to Salazar, a three-hour trip on winding roads. Don Teófilo would drive his truck knowing that the guards, realizing evangelicals were in it, would want to shoot on sight. At each roadblock, (Savage p. 11) [t]he burly driver leaped out and faced the crowd: 'I'm Teófilo Mesa. I'm a Conservative. These people have a right to live.' He glowered at the crowd as they silently looked at the ground, then one by one shuffled slowly off.

Arriving at Salazar the two ladies and the several men in the party raced to gather the belongings, throwing them hastily on the truck to make a speedy exit, never to return.

Accepting Joyfully the Seizure of Property   *Hebrews 10:34*

Meanwhile, the young couple was trying to guard the launch and the old hotel. Government troops forced them out of the hotel and raided the place, ripping open the mattresses, tearing the books to shreds (personal library plus Bibles, hymnals, etc. for sale on the launch), and scattering the debris on the streets. All was destroyed. Fortunately the young couple was permitted to stay in the launch at the oil company camp.

Wilf and Elizabeth had opportunity to put into practice the Scripture he had selected 14 years before as his life verses:

If ye then be risen with Christ, seek those things which are above, where Christ sitteth on the right hand of God.
Set your affection on things above, not on things on the earth.
For ye are dead, and your life is hid with Christ in God. Col. 3:1-3

Eventually they returned to the launch but because of the violence, TEAM asked them to sell it, and reluctantly they yielded. To combat the malaria mosquito the United Nations was spraying houses with DDT. The launch would enable them to reach some of the remote river villages. More than double the building price was paid to the mission and the launch changed hands.

The priest who had so energetically cursed it three-and-a-half years earlier now enthusiastically acted to reverse the effect. He lavishly sprinkled holy water on every apparatus, fixture, appliance. He blessed it and prayed there would be no mishap. Government crews navigated it about 200 miles (320 km) down river to load it. The launch sank—in its maiden voyage after being sold!

Watering and Reaping   *I Corinthians 3:6*

Furloughs for fellow missionaries ended and men with their families returned to Cúcuta, the safest place in that violence-ridden land. The Watsons felt constricted by the excess of missionaries living together forbidden by law to branch out, and the confinement of the curfew laws. Since TEAM's Venezuelan and Colombian fields were combined, Elizabeth wrote to the field leader and asked if there might be an assignment for them in Venezuela. The Barinas missionaries were ready to furlough so the Watsons, assigned to replace them, hired a large truck and crossed the border, without visa difficulty.

That fall Wilfred accompanied veteran missionary Gus Bostrom in his high-built Model A Ford to the plains, driving four days through countless miles of pasture land and admiring myriads of cattle, over trails which, most of the year, were covered with water. The final day they followed a trail beside the Apure River to Guasdualito.

The following year Wilf had to make the trip alone. Again the Lord provided through an oil company, which sold him a bargain of an old pickup truck. The first afternoon of that four-week trip the truck stalled in the middle of a river. Night was approaching. He could only sit tight. A storm upstream could be fatal. He tried to sleep but every strange noise caused him to fear that the river was rising. Praise God, it didn't. Early the next morning a big truck approached from the other direction intent on crossing right where the smaller one was "parked"—where rocks had been placed to aid in fording. Using his winch, the truck driver pulled Wilf's pickup to land and helped him recondition and start it.

After a stop for rest, food, and ministry with a small group of believers, Wilf continued up river to Guasdualito where he was welcomed by the elderly lay leader of this remote church. Augusto pulled a paper, yellowed with age, from his trunk. On the front page of the TEAM family periodical was his picture and story. He was so proud of his 20-year-old moth-eaten testimony that Wilf challenged him, "Brother Augusto, why don't you discard it, and ask the Lord to give you something new?" His testimony around town was "moth-eaten," too, but he *did* have a concern for the work of the Lord and urged Wilf to accompany him about 20 miles to a tiny village where some had recently come to know the Savior and were eagerly waiting for him to baptize them. Having been examined and approved for baptism by the church in Guasdualito, they were each joyously led by Wilf into the river for baptism.

"Now we want the Lord's Supper." They understood the South American evangelical custom: it's reserved for baptized believers in good standing with their church. "We have the bread," and they handed Wilf an Indian manioc cracker, "but no wine." Wilf wanted the only liquid available, water, to resemble wine so he soaked some red paper over night. It looked like mud! He added a bit of sugar and it tasted horrible. Instead of a chalice, all they had was an old empty beer can. Wilf could use colored sugarwater, but a beer can was too much! He wrapped it with a piece of colored paper and tied a string around it. Everything seemed to be wrong.

Afterward he told Elizabeth, "I have never had communion where I have felt God so close to us as with these people."

Bread Cast upon the Waters, Found   *Ecclesiastes 11:1*

After the Palm Sunday services Wilf headed his pickup back to Barinas. Merchants had been down in the plains and had all left before Easter. Wilf, with perhaps the last truck to leave, was hailed by two young women urging him to buy a turtle.

"Oh, I don't think so," replied Wilf.

"It's Easter week and nobody eats meat until after Easter. But they can eat turtle." Wilf hesitated and the other pleaded, "You're the last truck going out and we need to sell it."

Wilf looked at the captured creature, big as a wash tub, on its back with legs tied together. "How much does it weigh?"

"One hundred fifty pounds."

"What do you want for it?"

"Ten dollars."

Wondering what he would do with the giant, Wilf, easily swayed when it did not compromise his integrity, handed them ten dollars, saying, "But you'll have to put it up on my truck. I'll lower the end gate but I could never get it up there."

The three of them picked up that turtle and filled the back of the pickup with it. Three days later Wilf and his "pet" arrived in Barinas in time for the Good Friday evening service. Saturday morning they went to town and before long "Turtle" was the center of attraction.

"Want to sell it?" he was asked. "What do you want?"

"What's it worth?" Wilf had no idea.

"Will you take one hundred dollars?"

Wilf was delighted to let that big turtle more than pay for all the gas for the trip.

God Gave Them Another Heart

Milton Friesen, a Canadian co-worker, accompanied Wilfred to a jungle area formerly called *Juan Furia* (Furious John). Salvation had come and it became known as *Pueblo de Dios* or *Pueblo Nuevo* (Village of God or New Village). After an exhausting trek through steamy jungle, the missionaries, guided by two young leaders from the nearest church, were spotted by a youth stationed at the river crossing. Off he raced to the church with the news.

By the time we had trudged the final hour to the church, [Milton wrote] I was almost dead. A crowd of about 100 welcomed us with a special song, a poem, another song, Scripture and prayer. Then an old white-haired man welcomed us to Pueblo Nuevo. Amid hugs, greetings, and palm tree arches, I forgot all about my sore head and feet. Another welcome service awaited us at our hosts' home. The unannounced service that followed was joyously filled to capacity. After supper the believers reassembled from 7:00 to 8:00 P.M. We had more than 178 present and the response to the gospel was such as I have never seen before.

The next day, Sunday, [he continued writing his journal-like form letter] we seem like little kings here in a different world. We have just returned from the morning service and Wilf is talking to those who accepted the Lord last night and this morning. I counted 120 in the service this morning but people kept coming all the time, so I lost count. We really should have another service now for all those who came late.

Later: had a good chicken dinner—audience of about 40.

After a two-day side trip: here we are back in Pueblo Nuevo. What a blessing! The believers are on fire for the Lord and are a real inspiration to us.... The first service today lasted from 4:00 to 6:30 P.M—130 present; the Lord blessed. The 7:00 service had over 150 present and five accepted the Lord.

Wilf also united six couples in marriage. Two couples were grandparents and all had several children. All had been saved and married legally in previous months and now they wanted to have the Evangelical wedding as well. The women were dirty and barefoot, the men had long hair and beards. But all were happy in the Lord. It was funny to see them all in a semi-circle; one bride spit on the mud floor just before she said, "I do." After the service a white-haired couple elbowed their way to Wilf. The distraught pair, uninformed of the wedding plans, had wanted to be included. It was late; the service was over; a wedding was promised next visit.

Juan Furia was famous for a little four-inch figure made of red burntbrick called "St. Anthony of Brick." Being damaged, it was quite ugly but many miracles of healing were attributed to it. The owner presented "him" and other idols to the missionaries. "I'd like to take 'Brick' home," observed Wilf, "to show the folks at home the gods of these people and tell them about this miracle-working god."

"No," advised the junior missionary. "I don't think you should. Destroy it because if you take it, these people will think that you believe it has virtue and the power to heal and you want it to work for you. I think we should destroy it."

Wilf conceded and together they pulverized it and seven more idols.

> We drenched the whole outfit, [continued Milton] in kerosene and as the idols burned we sang, "Libertad, libertad" [Liberty, liberty]. After the evening service the whole crowd came with us to the house where we sang for another hour.... They all enjoyed it immensely, and although I was ready to drop, I did, too.

Heavy rains delayed their departure the next morning until 8:30. Several men accompanied them to the river. As they trekked along jungle paths, friends would emerge from their thatched-roofed huts for a final Scripture reading, prayer, and song. Of the final farewell at the river, Milton wrote,

> ...they hugged us and cried. I could not keep the tears from my own eyes, for the Lord has placed each one of these my brothers in my heart.

The Angel Said, "Follow Me"   *Acts 12:8*

A month later Wilfred was puzzled by a summons from the Barinas state governor which sent him to the governor of the adjoining state which included Pueblo Nuevo. With Elizabeth at his side, he presented himself to the governor in Guanare who accused, "You're the man who burned St. Anthony of Brick?"

"Well," replied the bewildered defendant. "Yes. The owner asked me to destroy it, so I did." A policeman was summoned to incarcerate him without a trial, without a bed, without decent food. What a blessing that Elizabeth was there! She contacted a local national pastor who helped her provide a cot and three meals a day for him.

For two weeks Elizabeth worked and prayed. She notified the Canadian Consul, the American Consul, the director of TEAM, and her former language teacher who had become a lawyer. They were all working to release not only Wilfred, but also the two youths who had guided him and Milton to Pueblo Nuevo and had been apprehended two weeks earlier. Milton also was on the hit list but his whereabouts were unknown to the authorities. The lawyer prepared a lengthy document showing that the false accusations deserved heavy jail sentences. Elizabeth presented it to a lower court judge who scanned it and, shocked, sent it to the highest judge. In short order Wilfred was called before the high judge.

"Are you the man who burned St. Anthony?" he asked, smirking.

"I didn't burn anybody. I burned a little bit of an image."

"You haven't broken the law. The bishop had you jailed. They kept it from me. Otherwise, you would have been out the first day. Go on home." Wilfred could see that the judge was no friend of the bishop. Although the two companions were not mentioned, they, too, were released.

Those two weeks in prison were no picnic and Wilfred didn't sing and rejoice. He was angry at that bishop who, clearly, was less upset about "Brick" than about losing that whole country area to the Gospel.

In retrospect, Wilf *did* praise the Lord that he was able to comfort and encourage his two companions who might have languished in that stinky mess had he not been there to facilitate their release. He was able to witness to other prisoners (none of whom were criminals) as well as to the guards (who were quite decent) and, upon his release, to present them with New Testaments. God works in mysterious ways His wonders to perform.

The Barinas congregation was earnestly praying for the liberation of their beloved, imprisoned pastor. Prayer meeting was in progress. Quietly the Watsons entered. Great was the rejoicing as the worshippers opened their eyes and rose from their knees. Again God had delivered!

The Spread of the "Missionary Rabies"

As we work on this book in August 1991, Mr. Watson is missionary and evangelistic speaker at a children's camp near Edmonton, Alberta. The Lord led him into this aspect of the work back in 1953 in the Peace

Northern Colombia and Venezuela, 1942-1954

River country. There, as here, he not only spoke in chapel, but also individually encouraged the children and staff to serve the Lord on the mission fields. One whom he encouraged at camp and again that fall at a missionary conference at the Peace River Bible Institute (PRBI) was the maintenance man, Curt Friebel, who had been a dormmate of Wilf's at PBI. In the letter Curt wrote for the benefit of this book he reminisced:

In the spring of my junior year at PBI I had rheumatic fever for the first time. After graduating, I worked at Prairie during the winter of '39-'40 as night fireman. Toward spring, I suffered a second severe attack of rheumatic fever simultaneously with pneumonia and appendicitis. After recovering, I joined the staff at PRBI.

The Watsons, on their second furlough, spoke at missionary conference. Wilf spoke to me about going to Venezuela with The Evangelical Alliance Mission. We discussed my medical history which had resulted in negative responses from several mission leaders. Wilf sought and received my permission to write to TEAM on my behalf. In less than a year I was on my way to language school where I met my dear wife.

We had over 30 years of fruitful ministry in Venezuela where I was involved in maintenance both of cars and especially of mission housing all over the field. I built an orphanage, churches, the Bible Institute, and buildings for our missionary children's school. For a time I was in charge of our printshop in Maracaibo. Over the years I did bookkeeping for various field ministries and served as field treasurer for a time. Eventually I was field business administrator, managing the mission headquarters building, coordinating missionary relocation and overseeing field construction.

I thank the Lord for using Wilf to encourage me to realize my missionary vision in spite of seemingly insurmountable physical problems.

In March of 1991 the Christiansen Academy, the TEAM school for missionary children wrote:

The School Board recently decided to name the MULTI-PURPOSE BUILDING in memory of Curt Friebel, a man who poured much love and expertise into Christiansen Academy. Besides serving as dorm parent along with his wife Emelia, Curt directed the construction of the classroom building and dininghalldorm complex. His love for children and diligent labor are ongoing testimonials to us.

Yes, the one with the "missionary rabies" had bit another!

Children Are a Heritage from the Lord   Psalm 127:3

An exciting highlight of the 1953 furlough was the addition of Florence to the Watson family. From the time Wilf was 12 and his sister Irene was born, he had taken an interest in children, and hoped some day to have his own. Before he ever saw Elizabeth, before they were engaged, she had informed him of her inability to bear children. Colombians tend to have large families and wondered why the newlyweds didn't have a baby and inquired how they prevented the pregnancy. During their previous furlough they prayed and worked to adopt a child, applying to several agencies in the United States, without a glimmer of hope. They despaired of adopting in the States.

Wilfred, traveling in Saskatchewan "biting" missionary prospects in early October 1945, visited a Saskatoon family with adopted children. "We wanted to adopt but the conditions are absolutely impossible," he told his host. "We'd need five times our income. We'd have to own our home. The agencies want us to stay where they can observe us for the first few years. No, it's absolutely impossible."

"Not so," challenged his host. "No problem at all. Go to Edmonton. See Mr. Hill, head of the child welfare. He's partial to Christian prospective parents."

"That's right," chimed in his wife. "We've gone there twice and had no problem at all."

Instead of returning west-southwest to Calgary where Elizabeth was with his parents, he traveled the same distance west-northwest to Edmonton and went directly to Mr. Hill.

"Yes, I'm sure we can get a baby for you, Mr. Watson. Go to Bethany Home—here's the address. I'll call the head nurse."

Early the next morning he phoned Elizabeth and said, "Sweetheart, get on the train and come to Edmonton. We're going to have a baby tonight." Without breathing a word to his mother, she took the 200 mile [320 km] train trip north to Edmonton. They went immediately to Mr. Hill who filled out papers for them and told them to return in the morning for a layette. Next day he gave them the layette and sent them to the hospital for their six-week-old son. All that night they traveled and in the morning presented Eric David Watson to his grandparents.

Some weeks later, farmer friends heard that the Watsons had a baby, born in August. Looking on their calendar they figured that Elizabeth and Wilf had been helping them in their fields just a day or so before the baby was born—and they hadn't realized she was pregnant! In 1953, seven-year-old Eric returned to the city of his birth looking for the baby sister Mr. Hill had promised his parents. However, the news media had accused him of selling babies to foreigners and allowing Canadian babies to leave the country. He was in a bind; he couldn't give them another baby. The three Watsons prayed and revisited Mr. Hills' office. Although reluctantly, he kept his word and released a baby girl for them. Like Eric, Florence Elizabeth was six weeks old.

In virtually every letter Wilfred Watson wrote, he copied or clipped and enclosed some poetry. Typical is this unsigned poem which he hand copied in 1937 and which expressed his lifetime sentiments.

Rather Go, Yet Rather Stay

Better far to be with Christ
   In the Glory Home
Yet I needs must stay a while
   On this earth to roam.

Love compels to wish to be
   By His very side;
Yet more love constrains for Him
   Here below to 'bide.

Not that place below I choose,
   Rather than His side;
But would rescue from the pit
   Souls for whom He died.

There are millions yet in sin,
   Who in anguish cry,
"Who will save us from the pit
   Ere we hopeless die?"

Others lie on beds of ease
   Cherish laurels here,
Spend their time on selfish gain
   Void of godly fear.

Though my eyes are fixed above
   Longing to be there,
I am willing yet to stay,
   Seeking Jewels rare.

Even thus 'twill not be long
   Till He shall descend
Through the air, to catch away
   Hearts that with His blend.

So while waiting in his will
   I will seek the lost
Whom he purchased for Himself
   At tremendous cost.

            Author unknown

Chapter IV

RESTORATION TO WEC: VENEZUELA AND COLOMBIA
1954-1970

The Lost Ax Head   *II Kings 6:5*

TEAM's regional office and home in Oakland—Elizabeth's home town—was vacant and the Watsons were privileged to live there and represent the mission. As Wilf traveled around representing the mission he was troubled by derogatory remarks about WEC: "It's so wonderful you left that mission that sends people to the field without support, and lets them starve to death."

"Congratulations, Mr. Watson, on getting out of that fanatical faith mission that won't let their missionaries tell their needs or ask for money."

"You certainly did well to get out of that nondescript outfit." On and on they went, running down WEC.

Wilf's conscience would prompt him, "Speak up! Tell them how WEC accepted you when you had such a strong desire to be a missionary. You had no money, no church, nothing to give them. No other mission would have you. You tried, but others wouldn't accept you. But WEC did! WEC asked you for $250 'seal money' and even though you had only $100 they still invited you into headquarters. Six months you stayed with them in Toronto and they never asked you for one penny for board and room. Those who ate there could put money in the kitchen box and sometimes the cook would report at morning prayers that it was empty. If you had money you would drop it in the box, but they never asked for it. They provided a needed winter coat. Before sending you to South America they bought you an entire outfit. They bought your ticket to New York and then to Colombia. In the three and a half years you were in Colombia with them, your supporters sent only $350.00 and the Toronto office sent you every cent of it even though the other missions always kept a percentage for office expenses."

His conscience kept pricking the silenced former WECcer. "Speak up! Tell them how your fellow missionaries pooled their income and shared equally with you. Tell about this mission that, quote, 'lets their missionaries go to the field without promised support and lets them die of starvation.' Unquote. Tell them how you were deathly sick in bed for six weeks and you had that tremendous doctor's bill, hundreds of dollars, and you didn't have one cent, and they paid it; they kept vigil night after night when you were so terribly sick. Even when you were leaving WEC to go to TEAM a WEC couple chose to give you her diamond ring for your beloved. Tell them what WEC did for you." Still he kept quiet. But, praise God, his conscience probed deeper and deeper. He thought about the son of the prophet whose ax head sank. He couldn't chop down trees. Wilf felt he had lost his spiritual tool by leaving WEC, and he wanted to recover it. The day came when he wrote his resignation to TEAM. He told them he had absolutely nothing but good to speak for TEAM—they had been so good to him. He explained how he felt about WEC—the mission which had helped him realize his boyhood desire to be a missionary when others would not. He wrote the letter—then tossed it into the wastebasket. He had a wife and children to consider. TEAM was his wife's mission. Her church was connected with TEAM. His support, also, came from a church which favored TEAM. Troubled in spirit, he went about his duties.

Elizabeth emptied the wastebasket and noticed the letter. Straightening it out she realized what it was and read it. "Honey," she comforted, "if this is the way you feel about WEC, I'm willing to join WEC with you."

Greatly relieved, Wilf rewrote and sent the letter. He had already been slated to speak at the TEAM summer missionary conference. TEAM leaders urged him to stay, assuring him that if he ever wanted to return they would be delighted to have him. The thought of Curt Friebel replacing him comforted Wilf as he parted from his dear friends in TEAM.

Following that conference, the four Watsons drove directly to WEC headquarters at Fort Washington, Pennsylvania. It was situated on a hill where George Washington had camped, five miles north of Philadelphia; hence it was named Camp Hill. WEC had recently purchased the abandoned, vandalized, dilapidated buildings and grounds of a military school—67 acres that were originally the elaborate summer home of a wealthy Philadelphia family. Because of the abominable condition of the buildings, the entire estate—woodlands, sunken gardens, castle-like main house and accessory buildings—was on the market for $150,000. The owner, being sympathetic to the mission, offered it to them for $60,000. The Lord honored the WEC no-debt financial policy. The estate plus cost of rehabilitation was soon paid for by:

    the sale of other WEC headquarters buildings;

$28,000 paid for three-quarters of an acre for the Pennsylvania turnpike;
$10,000 for top soil for "fill" off seven acres;
and two designated gifts of $8000 and $3000.

Thus, within about a year, the estate was clear without diverting one cent from contributions for the work of foreign missions.

WEC candidates live at headquarters at least six months to learn firsthand the principles and practices of WEC, and to come into fellowship with the WEC family—staff, furloughing missionaries, and fellow candidates. Lifelong friendships are formed as they integrate with WEC. Each staff member had a full time job with the mission, missionaries were treated like guests, and the housework for a fluctuating population of around one hundred, was left to the candidates.

The Watsons were housed in the rehabilitated military school dormitory and ate with the group in the castle across the way. Wilf had already served his candidacy in 1938-'39 in Toronto. There a dozen people had lived together and he had felt very much at home. At that time he had written to Lem:

> The living room, the radio, piano, and all is at my disposal as though they were my own. I go up town when I like and come in when I like. I can miss meals as long as I let the cooks know. My hours are my own. I have to stoke the furnace, remove the ashes, and keep the water-heater going, and then I make myself useful in any other way I can. I often go to the post office or run errands, mend furniture, or fix water faucets or any other little thing.
>
> The Lord is doing good things for me. The greatest is that which has affected my heart and soul. The Lord has given me a deeper experience with Himself than I have ever known. His love is taking over more of the undiscovered and undeveloped territory in my heart. He is answering, in a degree, the constant prayer of my heart; that I might be made a missionary. Not a Praying Hyde, a David Livingstone, a Ken Gray, an Angus Cunningham (I count these boys as real missionaries worthy to rank with the greatest), but just Wilfred Watson doing the whole will and plan of God for him.
>
> Just a word about material blessings. Yesterday I met a friend of WEC who gave me a Scrutiny Railroad watch with a solid gold case with a vest watch chain and two pocket watch fobs. It's worth $50 to $75. A Christmas gift from my heavenly Father.

Abounding and being abased in the Castle

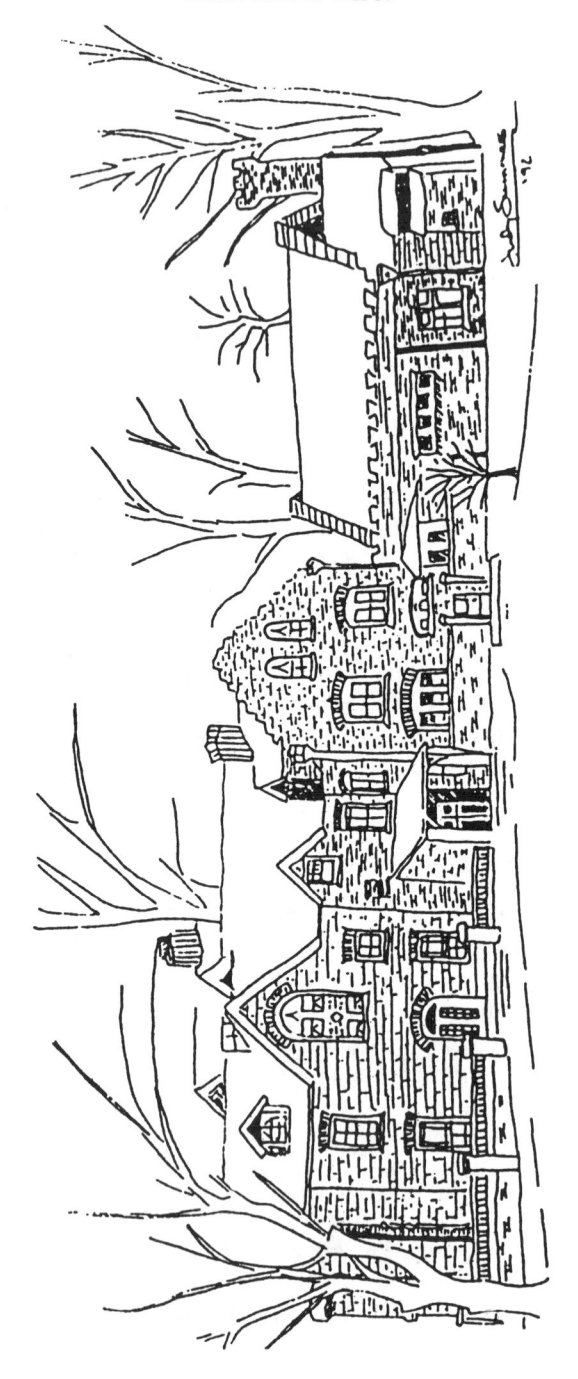

Before he went to Toronto his mother was concerned about his need for a heavy coat. Thinking he would return to the Peace River country, he had left his winter coat and was unable to retrieve it before heading east, so donated it to a friend up there. He certainly didn't have money to buy a new one. In Toronto, WEC introduced him to Mrs. Hines. Her son Ralph had just left for Colombia and she offered his overcoat to Wilf. It fit perfectly and was a much better coat than he had given away.

While in Toronto, Wilf enjoyed a productive ministry with poor children in a mission Sunday School similar to the Calgary Gospel Mission.

In 1953, the second time in headquarters, Wilf teamed up with other missionaries on a preaching tour while Elizabeth did cleaning and laundry and cared for eight-year-old Eric and baby Florence. Elizabeth passed scrutiny and soon the mission applied for visas for them to go to Colombia. The violence was at its peak and new visas were refused to missionaries.

The Ax Head Restored *II Kings 6:7*

WEC didn't work in Venezuela so the Watsons suggested entering it. Correspondence with three missions in Venezuela (TEAM, Evangelical Free Church, and Orinoco River Mission) suggested Barquisimeto, the third largest city in Venezuela, for pioneer church planting. It was the center of their districts but not being served by any of them.

Barquisimeto had three evangelical churches (not of the above named missions) so the Watsons settled far from any of them in *Barrio Nuevo* (New Suburb) and found a few Christians meeting in a two-car garage facing the street. Lacking a pastor, but knowing TEAM, and recognizing the Watsons, they invited the newly arrived missionaries to pastor them. The church grew like dandelions. Property was bought; a chapel built. People were saved and baptized. The work grew. Finances multiplied.

On the church anniversary in July 1955 a visiting, well-dressed lady with two children listened attentively to the sermon and responded to the invitation to accept the Lord Jesus as her Savior. Although she was from a Christian family, she had been living an immoral, self-centered life which was transformed that day. She was born again! This capable, well-educated nurse became a gold mine to the church, quickly becoming a leader in the ladies' work and secretary of the church board.

A graduate of the Assemblies of God Bible Institute who was seeking a pastorate visited the church. After consulting with the leaders of that denomination Wilf invited this fine black preacher to work with him.

"Our church is very poor," explained Wilf. "We don't have much to offer you, but we need you." Wilf and Elizabeth determined that any month the church could not give him as much as $100, they would make up the difference. That was barely a living wage for a family with eight children, but Julio accepted the challenge. He was a gifted and spiritual Christian. The church flourished under his dedicated ministry.

"Brother Julio," said Wilf. "This is your church. I'm not going to interfere. You know I live next door. Don't be offended when my truck pulls out just as you are starting your service. I'm going to start a new work."

When Julio took the church in 1955, 24 attended regularly, 13 being members. (Today his son pastors the 204 members. An indigenous Indian work near the Colombian border plus 26 satellite churches have been established.)

Members of that church assisted in the construction of a crude chapel on a lot which Wilf purchased on the opposite end of town. Then the Watsons began inviting neighbors—door to door or on the street. Some came, were saved, and were baptized.

As Wilf preached one night on John 3:16, God spoke to the heart of his six-year-old daughter. Florence believed on Jesus and knew that she would "not perish, but have everlasting life." The next week she asked the Lord what He wanted her to do with her life, so she could plan accordingly. He showed her He wanted her to be a missionary, a nurse, a wife, and a mother.

In contrast to the illiterate majority, a skilled dental technician and his woman dropped in. The Bible captivated him as did other books that Wilf loaned to him. Rapidly and accurately don Argenis assimilated the truths of the gospel. After marrying his woman they were baptized and the church was organized. Having heard Wilf's salvation testimony the new congregation chose to call themselves "The John 3:16 Church." As before, Wilf receded and left the young church, this time in the hands of the dedicated, enthusiastic and capable don Argenis. This church, too, flourished and produced daughter churches.

Being the only WEC missionaries in Venezuela could be lonely, so the Watsons rejoiced to be welcomed into the National Convention, an evangelical fellowship consisting mostly of TEAM churches. Wilf was elected chairman of the Evangelistic Committee to work with three other pastors who had so many other demands on them that the arrangement of evangelistic campaigns was left mostly to the chairman—who generally turned out to be the evangelist and musician!

To Wilf, those two churches in Barquisimeto, the evangelistic ministry, and the salvation of his daughter were a "definite seal of God on our going back to WEC and doing what my conscience told me we should do." As Wilf reflected on those good years in Venezuela he said:

> God was blessing us immensely because we obeyed Him, because we went back, cleared up our past, made things straight with WEC which had helped me so much when nobody else would. To our dying day we are going to give thanks that God gives the grace to go all the way back, twelve years walking in the desert. But we went back. We found our lost ax head (II Kings 6:5) and now we are chopping down trees, not with an old ax handle—our own abilities and Bible School preparation—but with the ax head of God, the blessing of God upon our ministry. That was decades ago and God is still helping us to chop down trees with God's ax head for His honor and glory.

A Gem Sparkles in the Desert

With the two city churches in good hands, Wilfred ventured into the poor mountainous desert. He found two forsaken evangelical churches and contacted their mother church which had abandoned them and now encouraged Wilfred to reopen them. Los Ranchos showed minor response; El Habra, less. But Wilfred plugged away.

Forty miles (64 km) he drove his pickup truck on the dangerous, sandy, twisty Pan American Highway; then three miles (5 km) on a dirt road to the river. Could he drive across it? It was deep. It needed to be tested. He waded in. His belt got wet. It was too deep. Back to the truck he waded, strapped his small accordion on his back, lifted his bicycle off the truck and toted them both across the stream. Cautiously, he kept the bike on the downside of the river so that if he tripped over a stone he wouldn't get entangled in it, and maybe drown.

Another four miles (6 km) he pedaled through the desert. As he pushed the bike in the loose sand that sultry Sunday morning, perspiring profusely, the discouraged missionary was praying, "Lord, You know I like to see things happen. We saw things happen in Barrio Nuevo and in the John 3:16 Church. We've seen a bit of movement in Los Ranchos, but I've been coming to El Habra for several months and nothing has happened. Lord, I ask You to do something today. Show me Your plan. Indicate whether I should continue coming here or not. If I don't get some sign from You, excuse me, Lord, but this is the last time I'm coming here." He was desperate.

He opened the church and dusted the crude benches. The few regulars wandered in, deadpan expressions without even a "Good morning" for the preacher. Approaching each one with a greeting, he received grunted responses. Most uninspiring! With the accordion, he led the singing. He prayed, read Scripture, and took the offering. All that was left was the sermon when a beautiful teenager with long black hair and white skin entered with two bashful little girls hiding behind her skirt. At the door she removed her walking slippers and donned a pair of shiny new shoes. Up to the second row she marched. She and her girls were the only ones near the front. As Wilf preached she nodded in agreement. "Is there anyone here," invited the preacher, "who would like to be saved and let the Lord Jesus Christ come into your life and give you the hope for life eternal?"

It was no surprise when this eager mother stood, raised her hand, and said, "I have come to be saved."

After the closing hymn Wilf invited one of the men to stay while he reexplained the gospel to Hilda. She couldn't read, but he opened the Bible anyway and read John 3:16 and some other verses and explained them to her just as Mr. Fowler had explained them to him so many years before. He led her in prayer, asking the Lord Jesus to forgive her sins, come into her heart, and save her. As they walked to the back of the church and he was locking up she said, "Would you come to my home?"

"Where do you live, Hilda?"

"Guaidí. About ten kilometers (6 mi) up the river bottom." Rain washes down the sandy mountains making temporary rivers six to eight feet deep (about 2 m). But most of the year they are sandy roads.

Wilfred considered the 6 miles (10 km) there, 10 miles (16 km) back by bike, wading over the river to his truck and then driving 43 hard miles (69 km) home to Elizabeth and the children. "Sister Hilda, if I can ford the river with my truck two weeks from today, I'll go and preach in your home."

Two weeks later the water didn't even cover the larger stones. Hilda was at the church when he arrived. The truck motor announced his arrival and the children, at least, came running. After the service Hilda inquired, "Brother Wilfredo, are you coming to my home as you promised?"

"Yes, Ma'am." One of the men of the church accompanied them, sitting in the back of the truck with the bike and accordion. Hilda and her little ones joined Wilf in the cab. Up the river bottoms and around huge stones they pressed incessantly, Wilf picturing that dear woman, dragging those little girls that long hot distance to find salvation. At last they saw her home, high on a bank overlooking the dry riverbed.

"Where will we meet, Sister Hilda?" Wilf sized up the 12 foot (4 m) square thatched mud-brick hut. Hilda and her husband had slung hammocks for themselves, their children, her mother, and her sister in the single kitchen-dining-living-bedroom.

"Under that big tree in the yard." The hostess had arranged log seating for 40 people.

"Lord, she must have faith!" mused the visiting preacher. "What a sight! People dressed their best emerging from the mountains, joyously greeting us and introducing themselves."

Hilda helped Wilfred with the singing as he led and played his accordion. He introduced a few choruses, read the Bible, and prayed. Hilda slipped up to him and whispered, "Brother Wilfredo, don't forget to give an invitation. Seven people are going to be saved."

Not realizing she had been talking with certain ones who had indicated their desire for salvation, he silently pleaded, "Lord, make it seven for Hilda's sake. She's a new Christian, Lord. Don't let her down." After struggling through the sermon under tremendous pressure, Wilf concluded, "How many of you want to be ready to go to heaven? Would you like to receive the Lord Jesus Christ as your Savior this afternoon?" With joyful release, Wilf counted just seven who responded, and afterwards reexplained salvation from John 3:16. How God answered that prayer two weeks before, asking Him to do something! Promising to return in two weeks, he jubilantly hurried home to share the thrill with Elizabeth, Eriquito (or, "Quito"), and Florence.

"Dad," said ten-year-old Quito. "Can I go with you next time? I'll help you with the driving."

"You're doing OK, Son, using those blocks that I've attached to the pedals. You could spell me off while I prepare my sermon."

During that summer vacation from boarding school (Wilf desperately wanted his children to have the educational opportunities he had been denied) Quito teamed up with his dad. Vehicles encountered were as scarce as the "Rules of the Road" out in that lonesome desert.

Next visit to El Habra the illiterate but enthusiastic Hilda was there with her tots. After the typical service, with just one live parishioner in the otherwise dead church, Wilfred eagerly loaded the truck and off they bounced to Guaidí. Again the people came and again Hilda whispered in Wilf's ear, "Brother Wilfredo, be sure to give an invitation. Five more are going to be saved."

Still not realizing how she had sown and watered the seed, he felt compelled to match her faith for five more. "Oh, don't tell me!" he thought. "I'll never survive. I'm going to have a heart attack." The frustrated preacher struggled with faith and with his jumbled sermon. But God was in it! Sure enough, when the invitation was given, five prepared souls responded and were led into the Kingdom of God.

"It wasn't the result of a sermon preached under pressure," Wilf later told Elizabeth, "but Hilda's humble efforts prior to the service. If I had preached on 'Mary had a little lamb' the results would have been the same."

Hilda requested a Bible. "Sister," responded Wilf. "You can't read. There's no school in these parts."

"Bring me a Bible," the woman of faith repeated emphatically. Having learned not to argue with a woman, Wilf complied and she paid for it.

"Brother Wilfredo, mark John 3:16 in my Bible." She had memorized it and began reading, putting her finger under each word: "Porque-de-tal-manera-amó-Dios-al-mundo,...." She went over it and over it until she recognized each word wherever she saw it in the Bible.

Next visit she asked for John 1:12—then Acts 16:31. She memorized the verses, then the words. Whether she ever learned to read anything else, she learned to read the Bible. She loved it! Oh, how she loved it!

The oil company donated frames and corrugated iron for quonset huts. One was erected in Guaidí. At the dedication, Hilda read a full Psalm perfectly. Wilf almost cried looking at that dear poor mother, a chosen vessel, beautifully used by God.

In answer to Hilda's prayers, an Australian missionary, Miss Joan Eley, went to Guaidí to preach and to teach. In April 1962 the church was officially organized with 12 baptized members. Thirty years later, Hilda, her husband, and their five children are walking with the Lord. Their second daughter has graduated from Bible School and she and her sister are both pastors' wives.

I Have Set Before You an Open Door Revelation 3:8

While the Watsons were enjoying a fruitful ministry in Venezuela, politics was boiling in Colombia with a 1953 coup and the overthrow of the democratic government. In the lull of political amnesty, persecution against the evangelicals continued. In *Hacaritama*, (p. 135) Elof and Isabel Anderson explained:

In the early days of his administration, Rojas-Pinilla does much to restore law and order, granting amnesty to all guerrillas. Many emerge from the "llanos" and the jungle to lay down their arms. However, the Conservative Party, the official party of the Roman Catholic Church, is still in power. One of the first acts of the new president is to do obeisance to the Roman Catholic Primate.... The Church hierarchy responds with its blessing, pronouncing the new regime Christian and legitimate....

A few months later there follows the historic decree that legally paralyzes all evangelical activity in the country. The authoritative order is entitled Circular 310, January 28, 1954 and reads: "Protestants are forbidden to make any public manifestation of their religious faith outside of churches and chapels. Protestants may not engage in any activity which might attract others to their faith."

New missionaries were denied entrance visas—and the Lord had led the Watsons to open up WEC work in Venezuela. Back in Colombia, continue their friends, the Andersons (pp. 137, 155),

.... an edict arrives closing all our churches along the river and prohibiting any Protestant services. Hundreds of priests are brought from Spain to counteract the evangelical advance...

The fiasco ... reaches its climax in "the days of May" in 1957.... The two parties [pledged] to work together for a restoration of constitutional government and embodied the concept of one or a series of coalition governments after the presumed end of Rojas' term in 1958.

By 1962 the resulting "National Front," a system of alternating parties and positions, downgraded the persecution from official to personal, and visas were being granted to new missionaries. The work begun in Venezuela rested in capable hands, both national and foreign. The hour had come for the Watsons to return to Colombia.

In Bogotá, field leader Pat Symes and several of his co-workers from 1943 along with new missionaries, welcomed the Watsons to Colombia. Eric had been left in Three Hills, Alberta with missionary friends, to complete his high school work. Florence was studying by correspondence with her mother. The Watsons were assigned to pastor the WEC church in Villavicencio (Villavo)—the gateway to the plains (which bachelor Wilf had known in the early '40's), and make monthly trips to the plains to continue the work of pioneer predecessors.

The unique, wirey, artist-translator missionary, Miss Sophie Muller, had introduced the gospel to Indians of the Colombian plains. The village leaders or chief often decided to follow Jesus Christ and to learn to read. The village would follow the leader. The Holy Spirit moved and word-of-mouth reports favored the señorita. Her Indian companions escorted her up and down the rivers while she studied the languages and translated Scripture. Villages that accepted her and her Savior were transformed.

After acquiring a rudimentary knowledge of a language, Sophie translated Scripture with the help of bilingual Indians. She taught reading using her own Laubach-type phonetic charts. She continued using a Christian doctrinal catechism so they learned God's Word as they learned to read. A new order of life was established. She taught them to begin their day with songs and prayers and to close it with a Bible study. She gave them a leader's manual so the elders could conduct Christian marriages, baptisms, burial and discipline. Any who did not walk right would be denied the Lord's Supper.

And she introduced semiannual conferences. Oh those conferences! We'll hear more about them later!

God Glorified in Sacrificial Love

Far to the east of Villavo in the Piapoca village of Corozal, the Watsons participated in one of those conferences. The closing day they were informed that a new-born baby girl was dying. The poor thing, born on November 22, 1963 (the day President John F. Kennedy was assassinated) with harelip and cleft palate, was unable to nurse. The concerned mother, sitting in her drab string hammock, was trying unsuccessfully to drip water from a wooden spoon into her baby. Elizabeth and Wilf took pity on the tiny one and offered to carry her to Bogotá to the WEC Clínica Emanuel (Immanuel Hospital). Realizing that if they held on to her the baby would die, the parents reluctantly released her, with the assurance that, if she survived, she would be returned.

Dropping the filthy rags from the three-day-old infant, Elizabeth cuddled her in the cleanest towel available and climbed into the jeep. From Corozal to Villavo, driving over prairies and trails, through wide, shallow rivers or ferrying by man-powered rafts, the journey took from one afternoon to the next, broken by short rest stops. After a torturous night in

Villavo with the unfed baby alternating between whimpering and screaming, Elizabeth bundled her up and, in a crowded communal taxi, carried her four hours up the mountain to Bogotá, ineffectively attempting to direct some milk past the opening of her palate.

At the brick wall entrance to *Clínica Emanuel*, Nurse Annie Noble welcomed the starving infant from the relieved nursemaid.

"What's her name?" asked Annie.

"She doesn't have one. She was born in the midst of our conference."

"I'll give her my own name, Anita. I'll make her my special charge! What's her last name?"

"We don't even know the names of her parents. She's from the village of Corozal."

"Then she'll be Anita Corozal."

Annie took the bundle of screaming lungs and hungry tummy into the clinic, cleaned her up, and put on a real diaper. The fight was on when the nurse attempted to force a small plastic tube down the resisting esophagus. Victory was proclaimed after a few drops of milk reached the deflated stomach and contentment brought sleep to the weary eyes. Elizabeth returned to Villavo confident that her borrowed baby was in good hands.

Five corrective surgeries later the "queen of the clinic," a beautiful, chubby, smiling two-and-a-half-year-old, was returned to the Watsons. When they attempted to take her to Corozal, their truck "died" on the lonely plains, far from civilization. They counted themselves fortunate that a dilapidated conveyance which resembled a tired school bus showed up which took them to Villavo for replacement parts. Returning, a half hour out of town the bus made a rest stop and most of the passengers exited for breakfast.

In accordance with common practice in that land of few gas stations where each charged more than the previous one, the crowded bus carried its own supply of gas. Gasoline trickled from the can behind the driver's seat, rolled down the aisle and made contact with a passenger's cigarette. With Anita on her lap, Elizabeth looked down and saw a ball of fire rolling between her feet. "*Incendio!*" she screamed, grabbed the child and ran. Fortunately she and the other passengers all escaped the inferno, but the bus and all baggage, inside and stowed on top, were demolished. Eventually they were able to obtain other parts and return to their truck and make repairs, but the time allotted to the trip was spent!

Multilingual, four-year-old Anita, was happily adjusted to her English-Spanish speaking parents and doting big sister Florence, conversing fluently in Spanish and jabbering more Guajibo than her foster parents. The Watsons loved her as their own and longed to keep her. Three problems loomed ahead: they were leaving the country for furlough and had no documents for her; they had promised her parents they would bring her back if she survived; most important, because of the centuries of Indian drastic experience with white men, was the total relationship of all the Indians with all the missionaries.

From Wilf's initial trip to Indian territory, with Pastor Pedro Moreno and his wife, Wilf had noticed that the Indian women consistently ran away from the visiting missionaries. The men were friendly and quite fluent in Spanish, so Wilf would ask them, "Why are your women so shy? Why can't they learn Spanish like you do?" No satisfactory answer was given.

"Look, don Pedro." Wilf indicated a small blond child. "She looks German."

"Brother," Wilf asked an Indian elder. "Tell me about this little girl."

"Her father is a tiger hunter. He hired some Indians as guides. He enticed one of our girls with a few beads, used her, and then left."

"Has this happened other times?"

"Brother Wilfredo, we never knew there were any good white [non-Indian] men until the evangelical missionaries came to us,— don Wesley [Driver], don Juan, you and don Pedro."

From early traditions to the present, all that Indians knew of white men was evil. From the sixteenth century their lands had been invaded by adventure-seeking, treasure-loving explorers, buccaneers, and priests, all on lengthy journeys without women. Self-seeking and ungodly, they used, abused, and kidnapped the women. The abnormal behavior suggested the invaders had come from an exclusively male society. The white man had exploited their land, game, wages, as well as their women. Other tribes of Indians had these same reasons for killing a group of New Tribes missionary men in the Bolivian jungle in 1948 and another team of godly young men who tried to evangelize the Ecuadorian Aucas in 1956.

Wilf later realized how important it was when he moved into Guajiboland that he was accompanied by Elizabeth and Florence.

Anita's family had received brief reports but no direct contact those four years. If Wilf kept the child, the family would have imagined the worst and the missionaries would have been classed with all other white men.

Counting on the family having their hands full with their other three children, Elizabeth packed a few of Anita's clothes, handed her a doll, kissed her goodbye, and sent her with Wilf. The secure little girl snuggled up to her daddy in a co-worker's pickup truck for the full day's joggle to Corozal. As usual, all the villagers gathered around the truck and Anita enjoyed the attention.

"Men, this is the little girl we took four years ago. We promised to bring her back, and here she is. We would like to keep her, but she's yours. You must decide."

The surprised father looked at the thin scar under the child's nose. Amazed he replied, "We were not expecting you. We are not prepared to give you an answer. After the service we will talk."

Anita understood neither the implication of the conversation nor the language of the children around her. A Piopoca, pointing with chin and lips spoke to her in Spanish, "That's your daddy over there."

Hugging Wilfred's leg against which she was leaning, she emphatically denied, "No! This is my Daddy!"

Another chin protruded: "That's your mother over there."

Another emphatic "No!" as she waved her hand indicating beyond the horizon. "My Mummy's awa-a-ay over there!"

Yucca and fish were served. Wilfred led the singing with his accordion at their usual vesper hour. He and his companion each gave a short message. After the service the father distressed the missionary with the decision to keep their little girl.

The Watsons loved this child as their own, and dearly wanted to keep her. However, Wilfred Watson, consistent with his commitment to doing what was right, sorrowfully accepted the verdict. "Everything is strange here for the little girl. I will hang three hammocks in the chapel, for her and the two of us. In the morning when we leave early she'll be sleeping in the chapel."

Before dawn Wilfred kissed his little darling goodbye and painfully set off for home. On the long trip home all the heavy-hearted man could think about was Anita awakening and crying, "Why did you leave me alone here, Daddy, with all these strange people?"

And scores of people have asked the same question. But Wilfred knew he had done right and shown the Indians that God's servants were different from other white men whom they had heard of or encountered. He hoped his integrity and that of the ministry would be underlined by this sacrificial act.

"This is my Daddy"

Elizabeth later wrote for the November 1970 WORLDWIDE THRUST:

> I was stunned when he returned without Anita. She had become a part of us. We visited her and found her happy and well-adjusted to her new primitive home. She was glad to see us and followed us around carrying her old toys we brought her. We pray that the Seed of the Word of God that we planted in her little heart will bear fruit in her tribe.

They That Feared the Lord Spoke Often One to Another Malachi 3:16

One of the converts whom Miss Muller had led to the Lord carried the good news to the Guajibos. His work was followed-up by WEC missionaries including the Watsons who attended and ministered at their conferences, those great spiritual, social feasts.

Six months previously a village chief had invited the Christians for the next conference. He and his men (maybe a dozen) built a temporary "sanctuary"—rows of poles set deeply in the ground with a steeply pitched thatch roof. They arranged rough logs for seating. Their women prepared bushels of manioc, a staple food made from the root of a shrub. For weeks, the men had fished and hunted and preserved the meat by smoking it.

On the appointed day, each complete village group appeared, bearing its own original flag (often just a piece of colored cloth), some food, and hammocks which would be slung two deep between the poles of the "sanctuary." As groups arrived, the hosts in a line welcomed them. These then joined the line until all had arrived and all had been greeted.

Meetings were held thrice daily. Each group, beginning with the hosts, stepped forward, led by the elder who introduced himself and his wife, who then gave her testimony. Then he presented each man who in turn introduced his wife, each one giving a testimony. Their children recited Bible verses and sang a gospel song. With 25 to 30 villages represented, and many villages taking an hour or so, the morning and afternoon meetings were filled. The missionaries, who barely deciphered a bit of Guajibo, participated in the evening evangelistic services. Wilf led the music with his accordion. Most of the people were Guajibos, but some were from other tribes, so every tribe would sing in its own language, then all together in Spanish. Sometimes they would say, "Now, Missionary, you sing it in your language." The Indians enjoyed the English "choir." Then the missionary had opportunity to give some new Bible teaching and reemphasize the importance of salvation. The women and children followed their men, and the men mostly followed the leadership of their chief. These group conversions were not the result of "easy believe-ism." Emphasis was placed on changed lives. "You can't go to those evil feasts you used to frequent." "We don't do that any more since Jesus came into our hearts."

What God Has Joined Together   *Matthew 19:6*

In the pre-evangelical era of the Indian culture, a young girl at adolescence was made the center of a celebration and promised to a youth. Prior to their union she was initiated—locked up for two or three days with the witch doctor. Wilf never heard any of the horror of those days but some of it was revealed to Elizabeth and Florence by older women. Normally, when they "joined up" they stayed together. She probably had a baby every year, most of whom succumbed to gastroenteritis in infancy. The mothers, who cannot tell how many babies they have borne, are old at 35 and rarely live to be 50.

A highlight of each conference was the marriages. The Watsons continued the teaching that Sophie had begun and encouraged the Christians to celebrate evangelical marriages, solemnized by the elders, which was recognized also by the Colombian government. The sequence of events was consistent: salvation, marriage to one's partner, baptism, discipline when deemed necessary (being barred from taking the Lord's Supper or participating in religious activities), then communion.

About two dozen couples had been living together. They had accepted Jesus Christ as Savior and Lord and were ready to be married. Most had been morally faithful to their partners for years and had children. Now they lined up at the front of the temporary "sanctuary" with their children in a big circle. A leading elder read the detailed wedding ceremony prepared by Sophie Muller *Jungle Methods* (p. 39). In song they recognized that it was God's purpose that people marry. Ephesians 5:21-32 was read by a deacon and another elder gave a message exhorting the woman to listen to her husband, and the man to love his wife.

> "This man must love his wife like he loves himself. No man looks angrily at himself, but rather he takes good care of himself. He gets food and clothing for himself. Likewise he should care for his wife. For her sake he leaves his father's house to dwell alone with his wife, that they might be one...."

Promises were made to be faithful and true to each other. "If she gets sick, will you pray for her or leave her? If she scolds you, will you pray for her or leave her?" The same was asked of the woman. The elders blessed them and prayed for them. The ceremony ended with a wedding song and the doxology.

Unitedly, at the appropriate times, the high soprano voices would chime, "I do." And in their turn the deep voices would respond, "I do."

Although the conferences were spiritual, an additional benefit was the introduction of unmarried people to those of other villages. The indigenous peoples of the world are being decimated by wars, violence perpetrated against them, famines, diseases from civilization, intermarriage out of the tribe, and intramarriage. In small isolated groups, close relatives are the only available partners and the genetic pool is being weakened. At the conferences people became acquainted with Christians of their own tribe or a neighboring tribe and good relationships were formed. Socially, too, they found encouragement and stimulation. After living with their small village of 25 to 50 people, it was great to gather with 300 to 500 in harmony and joy. The entire village would go to conference every 6 months, taking with them everything of value.

Disciples, Baptized and Living Godly Lives

Baptism followed marriage. Candidates would be examined by the elders regarding their understanding of salvation and consequent change of life. Questions from the *Leaders Book* (translated into English in *Jungle Methods*) might include, "Why is it that only Jesus can save us?" "How do we know that Jesus is God?" and "What does God say about our sins?" (Muller, p. 42).

The elders added their own enquiries: "Mrs. *Fulano*, [so-and-so] does your husband beat you?" An affirmative answer would result in exhortation to the man and delay of his baptism for another six months. "Fulano, is your wife good and obedient, doing her work?" Again a negative report would delay the baptism of the wife. The elders conducted the baptisms according to their *Leader's Book* (Muller, p. 43).

Florence, at age 13, having accepted the Lord Jesus as her own Savior and having dedicated her life to Him, wanted to be baptized among the Indians by a Guajibo elder. At one of the conferences, with her father on one side and the elder on the other, she was baptized.

Church membership automatically followed baptism. Membership in good standing locally or in another evangelical church was required for partaking of the Lord's Supper, in line with policy of evangelical churches throughout Latin America.

At the elders' meeting assignments would be made to prepare the elements as well as conduct the meeting. Simple manioc bread, their ordinary food, would be broken off as it was passed around. Grape mix was added to water for wine and served in *totumas* (emptied, dried gourds).

Although all attended the service of the Lord's Supper, the eligible ones sat in the front half of the "sanctuary." Wilf would lead the singing of choruses with his accordion; an elder would read Scripture in Spanish or Guajibo with explanation. Selected elders from the villages served the elements much as in other evangelical churches.

The next order of business is the missionary service. "Who knows a village which has not heard the gospel?"

"My cousin lives in *Tal-y-tal* [such and such place]. They haven't heard about Jesus. I'll take the good news to them."

"Who will go with this brother?"

"I will." And so it was arranged and the two were commissioned to take the good news to the village of *Tal-y-tal*. Armed with syllable charts, paper, pencils, and the love of Jesus in their hearts, they would set off to announce God's truth with the opportunity to learn to read about it in their own language. In receptive villages, they would lead the people to Jesus Christ and six months later would bring them to conference and the cycle of teaching, marriages, baptism, and the Lord's Supper would be repeated.

After the missionary service, all crawl into hammocks and sleep in peace until birds sing at 5:00 A.M. (Wilf doesn't need to check his watch.) At that precise moment a soft gospel song is heard. One after another joins until all are singing. In five minutes they are up and at prayer meeting where many lead in prayer. (This follows the custom of every Christian village, not just at conference time but all year, morning and evening. In their villages all may pray.) They read Scripture as Sophie had taught them, using the questions which she had incorporated into their texts: "Leaders read verse 1 and question women, then women read verse 2 and question men, then men read verse 3 and question leaders." (Muller, p. 33)

Following morning prayers, that final day of conference, if food is left, it's eaten. Carrying their belongings, all form a circle. Announcement is made of the location and date of the next conference. Then one after the other the village groups leave, walking around the inside of the circle, touching hands with each one as a gesture of farewell. For six months they continue in the things they have learned, anticipating the next conference.

Hospitality Guajibo Style

In 1964, seeing they could not do justice to both a city church and the Indian work, the Watsons relocated 200 miles (320 km)—some 18 hours of hard driving—east of Villavo in Guajiboland. Chief Ramiri, who with his village of Betania had already come to the Lord, offered Wilf about 5000 acres (2000 ha) of unsurveyed land. Wilf drew up a description of the boundaries which included six to seven miles (11 km) of twisting river and two creeks with sources barely 300 yards (270 m) apart which he enclosed with barbed wire fencing. With the description of this land, which he named *Emaús* (Emmaus), he obtained a government title and became the only property taxpayer in that vast area.

He asked the Guajibos to build him a native "sanctuary"-type building. With wife and daughter, plus all their worldly belongings in a truck and trailer, the 50-year-old adventurer-for-Jesus arrived just as the Indians completed it. The roof, thatched to the ground, extended three feet beyond the supporting vertical poles. It would later protect the mud walls. Wilf's immediate project was to trim the straggly thatch to neat bangs five feet (1½ m) from the ground so he could walk under it.

"Honey, I don't like this thatch on the floor. Let's clear it out."

As the obliging husband began removing it, Florence screamed, "Daddy! There's a snake! Kill it!"

"Is it poisonous?" asked Elizabeth. "Who knows? I don't ask if it's poisonous or not. I kill first, ask later," yelled Wilf as he swung his machete left and right attacking the battalion that had sought shelter from the rain in the unused house.

"Put the table over here! Get all the food off the floor!" Together they loaded the table with food and cooking equipment. There wasn't space for the sack of potatoes—a month's supply—so Wilf hoisted it on his shoulder, up a ladder to the rafters.

"What slid out of that sack?" shuddered Wilf. Fearful of losing his footing, he completed his maneuver, then looked down to see a snake which had slithered out of the loosely-woven sack. Down he jumped and attacked the villain. The Watsons found bed space up on the rafters!

Next morning as Elizabeth reached for the oatmeal can she jumped back screaming, "Wilf! There's a rattlesnake curled up right in the middle of the table!" Wilf's machete sent it the way of the potato snake.

"One more snake and I'm ready to go back to civilization!" The distraught missionary soon learned that cats were good watch dogs!

The next foe to fight was a tropical rain storm which washed through the house, a foot deep, carrying with it every movable object on the floor, and nearly toppled the house. The Indians helped fell tall trees, about a foot (30 cm) in diameter and placed them as a border about two feet (60 cm) from the house. Using Wilf's wheelbarrow, the Indians hauled in hundreds of loads of dirt which they packed around the logs, producing an effective barrier from the floods. Temporary thatched walls were replaced by dried mud-bricks, produced locally using a brick-press.

Besides building and improving the house and other buildings which Wilf requested for school and medical dispensary, the Indians proved to be delightful neighbors. Their village, Betania, was about 5/8 mile (1 km) from Emaús. Naturally—and happily—they were frequent visitors, but never until the sun was quite high and the foreigners up and breakfasted. Jungle acoustics carried the joyful sounds of children playing and the chopping of trees from Betania to Emaús.

"I am never afraid to leave Elizabeth alone here," reported Wilf. "Only Indians live within fifty miles of Emaús and they are mostly evangelized with some Christian Indians in each village."

All Your Children Shall Be Taught of the Lord   Isaiah 54:13

At the conferences, literacy was taught and those who had learned to read were encouraged to teach others throughout the year. But the children needed more schooling.

In anticipation of such a project and for his own family and co-workers, Wilf built an outhouse, dug a well, planted banana trees, 100 pineapple plants, and 100 other fruit trees.

School opened in 1964 with ten children from Betania and a WEC Bible Institute student who taught during his six-months' vacation. Before long there were 35 children enrolled—some walking, others arriving by canoe, and some living with the Watsons. Daily sessions opened with the radio tuned to HCJB and the Watsons' dear friend, Bob Savage singing *"Cantad Victoria"* ["V is for Victory"] and other gospel songs, the students joining lustily. They loved to hear Bible stories and the boarding students enjoyed additional devotional services after sundown. With the gas lantern and Wilf's accordion they would sit outside on clear nights singing and absorbing Bible stories.

Venezuela and Colombia, 1954-1970

The teacher taught the children to read and write in Spanish and an Indian elder attempted to teach them to read Guajibo but, being quite ineffective, was replaced by Miss Welthy Key, an American WECcer who had previously worked with the Cubeo tribe near Mitú.

Marcelo, son of chief Ramiri, was an exemplary student. Toward the end of his three years at Emaús, at age 12, he accompanied his father to sell their rice to a trader. Marcelo watched as they weighed the sacks of rice, calling out how many pounds: "Sixty pounds,...Seventy pounds..." The child recorded the weights of those 25 sacks then added them up to 1525 pounds. The merchant claimed there were 1200 pounds. Marcelo refuted the figure. Roughly belittling him, the swindler barked, "What do you know about it?" Marcelo produced the list. Examining his figures, no one could deny that there were 1525 pounds.

"Where did you learn that?" sneered the outsider.

"At Emaús, the mission school." That certainly didn't ingratiate the missionaries with the shyster traders, but Wilf rejoiced to be helping his vulnerable Indian friends.

Soon the Indians erected other buildings. When Florence was home from boarding school, she bunked with "Aunt" Welthy. Besides the teaching, Welthy helped with the boarding students, and the general work of the place plus occasional dental work. She was an appreciated companion for Elizabeth who often stayed home while Wilf visited Indian villages or made ten-day business trips to civilization. Welthy's Colombian companion was a great help with the housework, gardening, and animals. When Welthy left for furlough, Nurse Lois Pearson joined the team.

When the teacher was male, he bunked with the boys above the medical dispensary. A smaller building, erected for the girls, also accomodated the teacher those sessions when the student sent from the Bible School was a young lady. [See diagram, page 84.]

The Indians gladly sent their girls to day school, but hesitated to allow them to board. Priests, in former years, had enrolled them in boarding school. At vacation time all the boys had returned home. Some of the girls had been retained at school where they had delivered babies, and later returned, childless, to their villages. Suspicion turned to trust as the Indians learned to know and appreciate the missionaries.

During the first two years at Emaús, the toddler Anita was with them as a beloved daughter. Florence was there during vacation from schools for missionary children. Eric was in California, completing his education.

Emaús

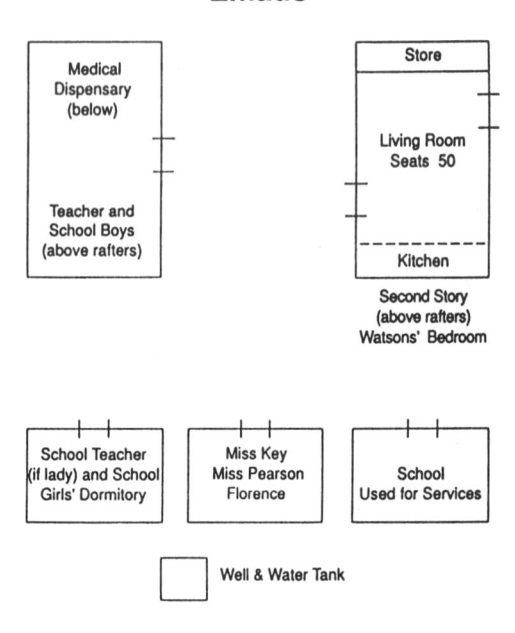

```
          Medical                    Store
         Dispensary
          (below)
                                  Living Room
                                    Seats 50
        Teacher and
        School Boys                   Kitchen
       (above rafters)
                                  Second Story
                                  (above rafters)
                                  Watsons' Bedroom
```

```
   School Teacher      Miss Key
  (if lady) and School  Miss Pearson       School
   Girls' Dormitory     Florence      Used for Services

                    Well & Water Tank
```

"What is that syllable?"

Prosperity and Good Health   *III John 2*

Clínica Emanuel, as well as several Bogotá doctors donated samples and other important medicines and Nurse Pearson was kept busy. The Indian children were often sick and die because of unhygienic conditions. To protect Anita who had been released from the hospital, the missionaries constructed a corral over a cowhide rug to keep her from undue contamination. Indian mothers who came to visit observed, learned, and followed suit.

The Indians made a big joke out of Wilf's building an outhouse but after hearing the exhortations on sanitation, some of the villages constructed their own. The hygienic teaching plus great quantities of donated medicines extended the lives of many babies.

A well with a gasoline pump and a tank and pipes provided good and convenient water which especially pleased the boarding students who enjoyed indoor showers.

A Guajibo, Manuel, described symptoms which seemed to indicate the use of some medicine in pretty green and yellow capsules which had been adorning the shelf, unused, for months. Apparently they helped, for the next day another from the same village requested the same medication.

"What's your problem?"

"I have the same sickness Manuel has."

"What is that?"

The vague response failed to gain the medicine—and it was so pretty!

A large quantity of tranquilizers had been donated. But nervous conditions were nonexistent among the Indians. A couple visited the medical dispensary and the man, speaking for his wife, complained of difficulty in sleeping. In Spanish, Elizabeth explained, "She is to take only one at bed time. If that doesn't work, she can have two, but never more than two." Then she summoned a bilingual to explain it meticulously in Guajibo. After further warning, she gave the lady six pills.

Unhappily, the Indian philosophy of medicine is, "If one is good, two must be twice as good." Next day the sorrowful husband returned. "My wife is dead."

"What happened to her?"

"Well, she couldn't sleep last night so she took all six pills."

The distraught missionaries could almost see the police converging on them with accusations that the unlicensed foreigners were dispensing medicines to kill the Indians! "Where is your wife?"

Polly wants to evangelize

"Two men are helping her, trying to make her walk." With a sigh of relief, Elizabeth remembered that the Guajibos don't have a word for fainting or passing out; they use the same word as for dying. The men helped her walk it off and she did survive. You may be sure, Elizabeth never again dispensed tranquilizers.

Many of those who survived early childhood reached about age 40 when they frequently succumbed to tuberculosis. No way could such patients be treated at Emaús, but Wilf did take some of the men to Bogotá, far away, to a different climate, to a different world with strangers. The trip in an unreliable jeep might be 24 hours in dry weather, twice the time in rainy season, and up to a week if the jeep got stuck in the mud. In contrast to the heat of Guajiboland, Bogotá is always chilly at night, about 40°F (5°C), and gets up to 80°F (27°C) for a few minutes on sunny days. *Clínica Emanuel* is surrounded by cement and high walls, with noisy city traffic on two sides. It has one concrete patio generally covered with hanging laundry. The confinement would be maddening for a Guajibo, and the treatment would involve a year or two. Some who were dying of TB made the arduous trip and returned robust. It was worth the sacrifice.

He Owns the Cattle   *Psalm 50:10*

In his later years, dad Tom Watson had improved his situation and at his death left $2000 to each of his three children. Wilf expected to be at Emaús for the next 15 to 20 years so decided to invest it there.

"We have 5000 acres of land," he told the mission leaders in Bogotá. "We have the school and medical dispensary but when civilization reaches us we won't be allowed to keep that much land for a mere school. That prairie land is useless for agriculture. For longer than anyone knows, the Indians have been burning that grass and the rains have washed away the top soil. Only tough grass will grow. Cattle can eat it when it's newly sprouted, shortly after a burning.

"What would you think of my buying two dozen calves to raise at Emaús?"

With the blessing of the mission committee, Wilf purchased 22 heifers and two bull calves which were transported in a huge cattle truck by a Christian friend. Prior to their arrival, he burned off about 200 acres (80 ha) of wirey grass, so fresh sprouts were on the menu when the cattle bounded off the truck. Periodically he burned more tall grass so there were always fresh sprouts for the cattle.

Two cattlemen ventured to the plains to inspect the herd. "Look at that! There must be sixty of those white Brahmans out there."
"God has blessed us. They've been producing well; mostly female. I've had almost twice as many, but I've been selling them to the Indians and teaching them how to care for them."
"Where do those Indians get money to buy cattle like this?"
"Well, I don't charge them much," replied Wilf, modestly. He almost gave them away.
"I've never seen any experienced cattle rancher with such good production."
"Those Brahmans are a good breed for this hot climate. But they don't give much milk."
"No, but enough for their children—and we have plenty for our Anita and our boarding students."
"Do you have other stock?"
"A bunch of wild pigs. They scrounge during the day and come home for some peelings and grain at night. They're pretty scrawny but when we butcher one, we stretch it over three or four days."
"Do you ever go fishing?"
"No, but the Indians do, and bring us fish. They hunt, too, and are delighted to sell us meat by the pound."

"Next-door neighbors" out there on the plains and jungles might live 20 miles (32 km) away, as did American cattle rancher, Ted Carlson. Wilf had heard about this bachelor flier, veteran of the Korean War, who, wanting to distance himself from all possibility of war, had secluded himself in Guajiboland. Although he had a plane and a jeep, he had chosen a horse to carry him the most direct route across the prairies, across the rivers, to visit the Canadian missionary. After the initial greetings, Ted launched into his business. "Watson, I have about three thousand head of cattle over at my place. I want to sell some of them, but you know, those big cattle trucks can't make it into my place. Can they get in here?"
"Sure do. We're nineteen miles from the road, but we have a good trail. Cars come in any time of the year. A big cattle truck brought twenty-four calves in for me a few years ago."
"Look, Watson, I can herd my cattle across the prairies. Could I load them at your corral?"
"Well, Ted. I've built a loading dock but I don't build anything very well; I'm too slap happy."

"Let me help you reinforce it." Both were happy for the companionship of another English-speaking man and they enjoyed working together. In a few weeks the trucks arrived and so did Ted with his herd of cattle.

As they worked, at the table, devotions with the school children, and in every activity, the Watson family life revolved around the Lord Jesus Christ. Earnestly, Wilfred presented the gospel of salvation to Ted. On another occasion while Wilf traveled about 60 miles (96 km) by motor canoe to visit an Indian village, he tied up his canoe at Ted's "port" and hiked about four miles (6 km) inland. He was pleased to see a 12-foot (3.6 m) square, one-room home—neat and clean.

Heartbreaks *Luke 4:18*

Florence had studied in a variety of situations: Grade 1 with her mother in Barquisimeto, Venezuela; grade 2 in the TEAM boarding school at Rubio, Venezuela; grade 3 in public school in California. When the Watsons went to Colombia, Florence studied at home with Elizabeth in Villavicencio. For grade 5 she was again in boarding school, a one-room WEC school, an hour's bus ride beyond Bogotá, with only five to eight other students. When that school closed she attended another boarding school, in El Llanito, sponsored by the Gospel Missionary Union.

Decades later, Florence left her five children with her husband in Memphis while she helped her parents in Alberta after her mother's surgery. She asked her dad, "What was the hardest thing you ever had to do as a missionary?"

Wilf's face reddened, tears welled up in his eyes and he unhesitatingly answered, "Leaving you kids at boarding school."

"Was it really? When I was a little kid, I thought you were just getting me out of the way so you could do your missionary work." Her thoughts flew back to that last time he had left her at school. She recalled having seen tears in his eyes, and was comforted to know that he really did care.

For three decades there had been a hurt in her heart. She had asked the Lord, "When will the hurt over boarding school pass?" She wrote to me, one of her boarding school teachers, "All that cold wintry night," in 1991, "the thought kept going over and over in my mind, 'Dad said that leaving us in boarding school was the hardest thing he had to do.' It was the key I needed to release those years of pain. As the hours passed into the next day, I realized the hurt was gone."

In 1968 Florence was delighted to be able to study by correspondence in Guajiboland. Her reminiscing recalled times when, instead of studying, she was learning to manage an outboard motor canoe, to spot a fish below the murky river water, to swim upstream. She was learning responsibilities in caring for chickens, ducks, turkeys, cats, and whatever other creature captured her attention. She learned to ride horses, milk cows, herd pigs to their feeding ground, and sheep to their pasture—such as it was out in the savanna.

Mother would fret that she was not studying but Dad simply stated, "There is more to learn in life than book learning." And she was learning more than nature and survival. She was learning to live with and care for people of another culture; she was learning to set her affections on things above, not on things on the earth.

When good friend Ted Carlson brought his cattle, the beautiful, vibrant sixteen-year-old captivated the lonely bachelor. On his return from marketing his cattle, he brought gifts for all the family. Florence loved life on the Colombian plains, and she admired her father's friend. She agreed to marry him. Visiting the Watsons became high priority for Ted.

"Watson, I've never met a girl that I wanted to marry like I do your daughter."

"Ted, you're a good friend, and I like you. But my wife and I have taught her all her life that she should marry a Christian."

Ted asked Florence for a Bible. She had an extra English Bible and, with her mother's approval, gave it to him. They suggested that he begin with the gospel of John.

Next time Ted visited, Florence was missing. Her parents had taken her suddenly to a small city, high in the mountains beyond Bogotá, to a sheltered school for Colombian girls and put her in the care of fellow missionaries with the instructions to guard her secretly. After arranging for a truck, Wilf and Elizabeth had returned with a Colombian couple to man the work with Nurse Pearson. They prepared to escort their daughter home and get her established in a high school where she could meet Christian young men.

"Mr. Watson, I've been reading the Bible and have stopped smoking."

"Fine. Did I tell you to stop smoking?"

"No, but I knew I should." The gesture proved nothing to Wilf.

"How can I prove to you that I want to be a sincere Christian, that there is no ulterior motive?" Ted had assured Florence that if she did not wish to marry him, he would leave her alone.

"Watson, I realize I'm nearly three times her age, but I want to marry your daughter. It's better that you give in because if you don't, we'll have to do it by force. I would like to get married. I can marry her. All my life when I have set out to get something, I get it. When I wanted to fly airplanes, I flew airplanes. When I wanted a cattle ranch, I got a cattle ranch. I want to marry Florence. It would be better to give your permission and let us get married without any problem than to resist it. If you do, all will be well. But if you won't..." The unspoken threat suggested kidnapping.

His parting words were, "How can I prove to you, Mr. Watson, that I'm sincere in my desire to be a Christian?"

Above the rafters, the Watsons stowed two mildew-proof, 55 gallon (209 L) steel drums containing their personal belongings. The truck came and Wilf and Elizabeth said goodbye to Miss Pearson, the Colombian couple, and the Indians. They expected to return within a few months.

In Villavo the police summoned them and inquired, "What's happening out there in Indian country?"

"I'm not sure I know," replied Wilf.

"Look at this newspaper."

"Wilf," whispered Elizabeth, horrified. "That's Ted Carlson." Shocked, Wilf examined the article which told of his friend, the one who had wanted to be his son-in-law, slain outside his little home where Wilf had visited him. Communist guerrillas had shot him in his doorway and left his body to rot, to be eaten by the vultures. Ted, being an American man, was first on their hit list. Elizabeth, American woman, was second, and Wilfred, a Canadian, was third. Had Florence been with any of them, she too, would have been murdered.

Wilf, who probably knew the country as well as anyone, supplied what information he had to the police.

It wasn't until the Watsons were out of Colombia that they learned that Lois Pearson, New Zealander, and the Colombian co-workers had been spared but that the beloved Chief Ramiri had had his arms tied with wire behind his back and had been shot.

The guerrillas ransacked the Watson's home and store and taken all they wanted. They broke open the padlocked steel drums and scattered the contents to be exposed to the rain and wild animals. The greatest material loss to Wilfred was the family Bible which his mother had brought from England and which had always fascinated him. As a small child he had delighted in the pictures and later read from it. He had gladly left all else from his parents' home to his two sisters, but he wanted that Bible. Not only was it a valuable keepsake but it had the full record of the family for generations back—births, baptisms, marriages, deaths. In recollection, Wilf reported:

That hurt! It was hard to be reconciled to that loss. But I am so grateful for Colossians 3:1-3. "Set your affections on things above, not on things on the earth." We lost thousands of dollars, including cattle and land, (we had to sell it at a loss to one who later made a "killing" off it), books and stores, but that old Bible, and an irreplaceable family picture album, which we would look at by the hour and which brought back pleasant memories—it was hard to lose those things. But once again we set our affections on things that are spiritual. As II Corinthians 4:18 says, "Look not at the things which are seen, but at the things which are not seen: for the things which are seen are temporal; but the things which are not seen are eternal." Thank God we look at the things that are not seen because they are eternal; things that we love and appreciate and strive to obtain.

Chapter V

REPRESENTING WEC IN USA: 1970-1978

He Heals the Brokenhearted   *Psalm 147:3*

After the personal turmoil in Colombia, the Watsons sought emotional and spiritual renewal at Maranatha, a summer conference grounds in Michigan founded and directed by Dr. H. H. Savage. He was pastor of Wilf's supporting church and father of TEAM missionaries, Bob (who had earlier solicited aid on Wilf's behalf) and Jim (co-worker in Venezuela). Rather than carrying on a heavy speaking and traveling schedule, they found it better to do manual work, to have family time, and to sit under the ministry of the outstanding conference speakers. Wilfred was handyman, Elizabeth worked in the kitchen, and Florence waited tables. The remuneration beyond room and board was small, but the Watsons found it to be adequate.

During the winter they served as caretakers, occupying one of the winterized cottages rent-free. This provided a comfortable home, allowed Florence to attend high school, and Wilf to go on speaking engagements for WEC. In contrast to the strenuous summer work, the winter work was light and no money was paid them by the conference grounds.

Florence's first encounter with snow, walking to a Michigan public high school with boots, scarf, and a heavy coat gave way to spring.

God's Thoughts Are Not Wilf's Thoughts   *Isaiah 55:8*

Spring Conference at WEC's Camp Hill brought furloughing missionaries together with the home base staff. First item of business, as always, was worshiping their Lord and seeking His face. Items on the agenda included promoting interest in worldwide missions in churches and individuals, recruiting candidates, and strategically placing personnel. These and other matters were discussed, prayed over, and decided.

Elwin Palmer, North American Director, and John Capron, Director of Home Ministries for WEC in North America, both Mississippians, presented their burden at the meeting. "I've been making forays into the South these past few years," began John. "The time is right for WEC to break into the Bible Belt."

"Yes," responded Elwin. "We haven't been reaching the Bible institutes, colleges, and seminaries throughout the entire mid-south. Memphis, Tennessee would be a good central location."

93

"We need an experienced missionary couple, someone with enthusiasm, ... dedication to missionary work."

"Wilf," said John, "You visited Seaton's church there in Memphis with me. There's a pastor with a heart for missions. That church responded so well to your challenge. Will you and Elizabeth pray about representing the mission there? You have the missionary rabies and have been biting prospects for years."

"We're getting ready to return to Colombia," objected Wilf. "Maybe back to Emaús, or at least some place in South America."

"Your ministry could be multiplied and spread over the whole wide world," challenged Rusiko who had first brought Wilf into WEC. "Few young people have the vision and dedication to serve the Lord with or without money. You could go into those churches and schools, get prospects on the fly-paper, and give them a good bite. You've already been infecting people with those missionary rabies for a long time. It seems you would be the best ones to settle in Memphis and recruit missionaries and prayer support."

Wilf thought of the young people from the Peace River country whom he had "bitten" and they had served the Lord in Africa, Indonesia, Venezuela. He thought of Ross Clemenger whom he had visited in Alberta and then with a follow-up letter had encouraged to go to Colombia. Washington Padilla was serving the Lord in Ecuador and the young people of La Donjuana, whom he had encouraged, had gone to Bible School and into the Lord's service.

On and on he thought of people from four countries whom he had "bitten." Yes, he *did* have the "missionary rabies."

Privately he discussed it with Elizabeth. "Sweetheart, I'm all set to return to Colombia. Or at least, somewhere in South America. How about you?"

"I'm ready to go wherever you go. You've always been willing to listen to others, especially those who are over you in the Lord."

"Yes, I do want to be obedient. But it's hard to see this as the Lord's will." They prayed about it and considered the matter; they chose to submit to the mission leadership.

God Gives Grace and a Home

Florence had a few more weeks of her school year so while she stayed with friends in Muskegon, Michigan, her parents loaded up the old van and the second-hand 'bug' and drove to Memphis, where Mrs. Isabel Henrich graciously welcomed them into her attractive home.

That first Wednesday they visited Southmore Baptist Church where they knew the interim pastor, an outstanding Christian gentleman and a prosperous business man. At the prayer meeting, Mr. Ed McAteer greeted the WECcers and said, "Brother Watson, would you like to give a testimony and tell us your plans? I know you belong to WEC and so you can't tell us your needs but anyway, prayer requests."

Wilf chafed at the implication that it was WEC law, rather than his personal conviction, that he pled his financial needs to the Lord alone. But he graciously told of the Lord's leading and mentioned that he and Elizabeth were looking to the Lord for a home suitable for a regional WEC headquarters. The group prayed with them for this need.

The next day Mr. McAteer phoned Wilf. "One of our members has a proposition he would like to make to you. Could you meet him tomorrow at 1611 Mary Drive in Memphis?"

"Sure, I can."

At the appointed time, the Watsons met with the Keith-Mohundro family, all outstanding Christian people.

"Mother went to be with the Lord a year ago," began Mrs. Mohundro. "Dad is in poor health and misses her so much."

"He's a big man and spends much of his time in bed," added his son, Alton Keith. "Would you consider living with and caring for our father? We will pay for the utilities, the food, and his other expenses. A reliable family friend, a dear black lady, comes once a week to clean the house and will be available at other times in case of emergency."

"We'd like to meet your father."

"Of course. He can hear, but his speech is limited. We'll go two doors down and visit him."

After they talked and prayed together, Wilf said, "We appreciate your offer. This is a lovely home. We want to talk it over, and consult with our mission leaders."

Entering the car, he said to Elizabeth, "I never thought I'd be nursing an elderly man!"

"We'll pray about it, Honey, and see what God says to us."

Two days later he called Camp Hill and talked with John Capron. "John, this is Wilf here in Memphis."

"Bless you, Brother. How are things going?"

"You know Mrs. Henrich?"

"Mrs. WEC of the Mid-south!"

"The same. She is giving us the most wonderful hospitality!

"John, we've just been visiting with the family of an elderly gentleman who needs care. He's living in his three-bedroom home. His family would like us to occupy it and care for him. They'll pay the utilities and, of course, all his expenses."

"How old is he and what's his condition?"

"He's eighty-two. He's in bed most of the time. He needs help getting up and the lady who has been caring for him finds him too heavy to handle. He has two daughters nearby, but they have both had back trouble and can't handle him."

"How does Elizabeth feel about it? And how do you feel about it?"

"John, we don't have our parents. We weren't privileged to care for any of them when they needed us. Here is a godly octogenarian who needs help. Maybe the Lord will let us compensate for our unavailability to care for our own, by sort of adopting him as a father, and taking care of him. John, we'd like to do it, but if you feel it would interfere with our ministry, we'll acquiesce."

"You're just getting started. You don't have commitments, yet. It looks like a provision of the Lord. Go for it!"

The family offered to provide groceries which the Watsons refused. They *did* accept the cleaning service, help so Elizabeth could get out, and contributions to WEC. For five months Elizabeth, Wilfred, and Florence tended and loved the old man. At his homegoing, the family sold the house to WEC advantageously.

Opening Doors for Wec

The young Mr. Keith introduced them to the newly established Maranatha Bible Church pastored by Mr. Randolph. Sacrificially, the congregation had purchased a house and remodeled it for services. Attracted by their resolve to give 50% of their church income to missionary work, Wilfred stated: "That's where I want to be. I want to be there and help them get started."

That year, 1971, WEC set "76 by 76" as one of its goals, meaning they would pray and work toward commissioning 76 new missionaries by the year 1976. As members of the recruiting team, the Watsons were to visit schools and churches. They enjoyed fellowship with many fine churches such as Minnick Bible Church, Tchulahoma Baptist Church, and Haven View Baptist Church where they continually presented missionaries. Many denominational churches were interested in missions, had given generously to the cooperative denominational program, but had never seen a live missionary. How thrilled they were to actually meet some: Dr. Helen Roseveare of Zaire, Len Moules of Nepal, Miss Daisy Whaley—a black Philadelphian missionary to Ivory Coast. She was lovingly accepted and greatly appreciated by the white congregations in the mid-south. One lady in Missouri reported, "We saw Christ in her face and heard Christ in her words." Then there was Miss Joan Eley the Austrailian sheep-rancher who took over the work in Guaidí with Hilda; and scores more.

In 1972 the mission asked Wilf to schedule two weeks for Leonard Moules, their International Secretary (Director), formerly a missionary to the India-Tibetan border. Wilf guided him to Mid-South Bible College, Dallas Bible College, LeTourneau College in Longview, Texas, other schools, and churches. At the end of this tour Mr. Moules said, "Wilf, never in all my life have I been run so hard. But I enjoyed every minute of it!"

Dr. Helen Roseveare, the English medical doctor who had been captured and abused in the Simba revolution in the Belgian Congo (now Zaire) in 1964, accompanied Wilfred for a month to schools and churches in Texas, Missouri, Arkansas, Tennessee, Alabama .... One Sunday evening she was scheduled to speak at the Northside Bible Church in Memphis. The previous week she had given her testimony to about 500 Southern Baptist pastors at a luncheon. Dr. Adrian Rogers, former president of the great Southern Baptist Convention and pastor of the huge Bellevue Baptist Church in Memphis, was present. He approached Wilf afterwards. "Brother Watson," he said, "I must have that lady in my church on Sunday night."

"Doctor Rogers," replied Wilf. "I'm sorry, but we have her booked at a small church where there might be less than fifty people. I would love to take her to your church where I know there would be anywhere from two thousand to twenty-five hundred people. But it's a policy of mine to keep commitments. We can't deny those people on the northside the privilege of having Dr. Roseveare in their church."

"What time does she speak there?"

"It's from six to seven."

"Our service begins at six thirty. Would they let her speak first and then let her come here?" Thus it was arranged that Dr. Helen presented the challenge of missions at both churches.

When Mr. Randolph graduated from Mid-South Bible College, his church asked Rev. Watson to join the ordination council. To Wilfred it was a joyous blessing to help his dearly loved pastor. Adding to his excitement and joy was the realization that the council would be chaired by retired pastor of the Bellevue Baptist Church, Dr. Robert G. Lee. "Just think!" he said to Elizabeth. "They've asked little me to be the scribe for the council!" It was an unforgettable experience.

One of the many churches that always welcomed WEC missionaries was the Willow Park Baptist Church, pastored by the Reverend John Seaton. The charming daughter of the WEC representatives was occasionally asked to sing. In the congregation was the pastor's son, David, a graduate of LeTourneau College in Longview, Texas. Before long it was Wilf's happy privilege to assist Pastor Seaton in the marriage of their children. Florence, who had been infected with the missionary rabies by her father, bit her crop-dusting pilot husband and before long they applied to and were accepted by the South America Mission for jungle flying in Bolivia. While David studied Spanish in south Texas, Florence enrolled in the Spanish language Bible Institute on the same campus.

Rendering to Caesar   *Matthew 22:21*

"Wilf, what's this?" Elizabeth was examining the mail.

"Hmmm. They're calling me in for an IRS audit. Well, I'm not afraid. Our papers are all in order. They won't get much from our small income. I'll give them a call."

The schedule was set for the audit. "Good morning, Mr. Watson. Thank you for coming into the Internal Revenue Service. I'll pull your file."

"Here are my papers since I came into the country three years ago. I haven't earned enough to pay much tax."

"We have no problem with your income tax, Sir. But you are not paying Social Security Tax."

"I realize that. I'm considered self-employed. I'm an alien in the United States. I don't intend to remain in this country."

"Oh, but you must pay Social Security tax currently as well as for the past three years, since 1971. Also there will be penalties for non-payment and interest on what you owe. I'll check the computer and come up with a figure." Wilfred was shocked into silence at the four-digit figure.

Angry and fighting mad, Wilf called WEC headquarters. "Elwin! I've got to get out of this country. Let me go to Canada or to Colombia. I want to get out of the United States."

"Calm down, Brother. What's the matter?"

"They've just assessed me over a thousand dollars for Social Security since 1971. That system won't last ten years. It's just money down the drain. I don't have any money except what God's people give. I don't want to divert one cent from foreign missions. Elwin, I don't want to pay Social Security tax. I want out of here." Wilf was kicking like a steer.

"Hang in there, Wilf. We're delighted with the work you're doing in the mid-south. No section of the United States has increased their interest in and support of our missionaries in the past *ten* years like your area has in the past *three*. You stay right where you are. We will pray with you and the Lord will provide."

Reluctantly Wilf backed off. God did provide. The debt was paid. He was sure he would never see that money again.

Four more years the Watsons represented WEC throughout the mid-south. Retirement age arrived. Checking with Social Security, they learned that Maranatha Conference Grounds had paid into the fund not only as they worked hard all summer, but also that winter when they served as caretakers and earned their rent. Years before, First Covenant Church in Oakland, California had also paid into it for a year. They were just a few months short of the 40 quarters required to draw benefit from Social Security, and they could send payments to complete the requirements. They also learned to their delighted surprise that they could live any place in the world and still receive payments the rest of their lives. Shortly after turning 65 they began receiving $300 per month and within two years they recuperated all they had deposited. Later the benefits increased.

They began writing to their supporting churches:

> Don't send us any more money. Give it to younger missionaries who need it more than we do. Write to us, pray for us, let us visit you, but don't send us money.

Some of the churches removed them from their budget, others reduced the amount, but some insisted on sending the full support. What a blessing in disguise!

Chapter VI

CHURCH PLANTING AND DEVELOPMENT: VANCOUVER AND BOLIVIA:1978—

Knowing How to Abound   *Philippians 4:12*

The Watsons requested an assignment to Colombia, Venezuela, or any other Spanish-speaking country. However, WEC being reluctant to return missionaries to foreign countries after age 65, the Watsons decided to retire in Vancouver, British Columbia. Their July 1978 form letter detailed their move.

>We saw more tears and had more farewell parties leaving Memphis than we had all five times we went to South America. One church has sent us support since we are here and a dear soldier boy has sent to us every month. Things are expensive here ... but U.S. dollars are worth $1.12 Canadian so we are very well off indeed. Praise the Lord.
>
>We entered Canada pulling an old U Haul trailer behind our eight-cylinder '68 sedan. Immigration officers asked how long we were going to be in Canada and we said, "for twenty-five years." They were so good to us and neither charged us duty nor even looked at our things.

Settling in Vancouver, other blessings awaited them. The Canadian Old Age Pension notified them that they were each entitled to $200 per month. "We were really in the dough," said the repentant Wilf, recalling his earlier anger at the Social Security system.

For many years the Pontiac Baptist Church had set aside monthly retirement funds to which the Watsons had added birthday and Christmas gifts. The accumulation, placed in an annuity with Prairie Bible Institute, amounted to about $35,000, which they withdrew to purchase a home near Vancouver. Remembering the Great Depression, never having been in debt throughout his missionary career, and fearing it like a viper, Wilf selected minimal housing for $40,000 rather than take out a mortgage. They were delighted to have their own home, and after doing some repairs and an addition, it was comfortable and satisfactory. However, at resale time they regretted not having taken a mortgage to purchase a more substantial building.

Wilf never forgot his first years in Colombia when other missionaries shared their scanty support money with him. He was thrilled to use his abundant supply to encourage several younger missionaries who had limited finances, saying, "We were so glad we could show our gratitude to the WEC who had helped me realize my boyhood ambition in 1938, giving me my outfit, complete passage to Colombia, and financial support when I had no other source of help."

... And Thy House Acts 16:31

Retired missionaries from Colombia welcomed the Watsons to their fellowship and introduced them to Spanish-speaking immigrants, some of whom were enjoying a Monday evening Bible study. Since the area lacked a Spanish church, the Watsons encouraged this group to organize. A large active church rented them facilities.

Announcement was made on a Spanish-language cultural radio program of the *"Iglesia Evangélica de habla espana"* (Evangelical Church that speaks Spanish), to which the Tirado family from Medellin, Colombia habitually listened. Mrs. Tirado's recently saved mother, doña Alicia, had traveled from Miami to Vancouver to share the good news with her family. Excitedly she asked her son-in-law to call the radio station for details. At the next service, in walked the grandmother, her daughter Gloria, the two children, and their father. Upon entering, doña Alicia, recognizing the same Spirit she had known in Miami, raised her arms and exclaimed, *"Alleluia!"* Wilf in the pulpit rejoiced at the presence of a new kindred spirit.

The Tirado family invited the Watsons to their home the next evening for a Colombian meal. Doña Alicia fasted all day while preparing the food. She served the guests with Gloria and Constantino while the children played in another room. After the scrumptious meal, Wilfred, as was his custom, pulled out his New Testament. Opening to Luke 15:11-24, he read the story of the prodigal son and then turned to Gloria and asked, "Wouldn't you like to return to the Father as did the prodigal son?"

With tears washing her make-up down her face, she sobbed, "Yes, I do." Even as Mr. Fowler had led him in the prayer of repentance and salvation years before, Wilf now led Gloria Tirado to the feet of the Savior.

Then, turning to her husband, he said, "Don't you want to do what Gloria has done?" Refusing the invitation, Constantino began to explain how he had lived a bad life, and he had to improve before he could come to God. Turning to Revelation 3:20, Wilfred read, "'Behold, I stand at the door and knock, if any man hear my voice and open the door I will come in to him and sup with him.'"

"He's knocking at your door, now. Your refusing Him is making the situation worse."

"Okay. I'll accept Him now." With another glad shout of "*Alleluia!*" Alicia rushed in and hugged her daughter and son-in-law.

Beginning the following Monday, the Watsons met with their new children-in-the-faith for weekly Bible study and discipleship training.

In Season, Out of Season　　　　　　　　　　　　　　　*II Timothy 4:2*

Florence and David Seaton, with Elizabeth Jane and Deborah June, had been in Bolivia a year when they expected their third child. The grandparents wanted to welcome the baby, so early in February 1979 they flew to Santa Cruz where the South America Mission (SAM) had its headquarters and flight center.

As they cleared customs, the officer stamped their documents. Knowing how difficult it is for missionaries to obtain visas, and expecting to see a 30 day visitor's permit, Wilf was amazed when he opened his passport. "Well," he said, "I guess the Lord has work for us to do here. We can stay here for two years!"

Baby John Wilfred barely preceded his grandparents to Bolivia, and was home with his mother to greet them. Big sisters were four and two and Mommy was delighted to have her parents' help for a full month. Mormor (Swedish for mother's mother), stayed close to home but Granddad was most gratified with several opportunities to preach—in town, and even in a flooded Indian village to which David flew him. He was impressed with the rescue of a poor Indian woman who was hemorrhaging after a miscarriage, whom David transported to a hospital, saving her life. At the end of their stay, they wrote:

> We are just bubbling over with love and gratitude to the Lord. We express ourselves with Psalm 126:2, 3. "Then was our mouth filled with laughter and our tongue with singing ... the Lord hath done great things for us whereof we are glad."

Carnival is just before Lent. It is customary to go wild with pleasure and sin. Dance bands played all night on Monday and Tuesday. On Monday they threw water on any who ventured outside their homes. On Tuesday they threw paint and mud. Anyone outside wore old clothes and was soaked with water and/or paint and/or mud. What a mess! We stayed in and enjoyed a secluded visit with our family. The next day (Ash Wednesday) they go to church and confess their sins then they do not sin again until 40 days later (?), during Lent, which ends with Good Friday. We are so grateful to you for helping us go to Bolivia. Bless you.

That two year visa couldn't be wasted! They were in a Spanish-speaking country with adequate support from the United States Social Security, Canadian Old Age Pension, and gifts from several churches and individuals. However, they were not prepared to remain so returned to Vancouver to continue working with their Spanish-speaking church, promising to return.

Pruning, Nurturing, and Growing   *John 15*

The Vancouver church which grew to 20 members declined to 15, about half of whom had been saved and baptized there. The congregation tended to be middle-class, from eight Latin American countries. Pastor Watson was disappointed in the lack of response to his careful teaching of tithing as a God-given opportunity to grow in grace, In October, 1979, he wrote:

> Had they been saved in their homeland where their income would have been minimal, they would have found it much easier to tithe. Formerly surrounded by the "have-nots of the world", now by "the haves", they want to *have right now*. With credit cards, car loans, and mortgages they can have two cars and a $65,000 home fully furnished but their five-figure incomes cannot be stretched to give more than ¼ to ½ of 1% to the Lord. I almost cried when the treasurer told me he took only two dollars out of the offering box one Sunday and only five the previous Sunday. We have an offering box at the back of the church to try to practice Matthew 6:3, 4 and to encourage our folks to give *to the Lord* and not to men, but it is not successful yet.
>
> They pay $50 a month rent and in January started giving me $100 a month for car expenses and very recently started giving $100 a month to three foreign missionaries in South America. Pray that they will learn to "sow abundantly" so that they will "reap abundantly" according to 2 Cor. 9:6. We will refuse our part before we will allow them to fall down on their missionary commitment.

Watsons lived 17 miles from the church, and visited members living as far as ten miles in the other direction so travel expenses amounted to more than the $100. Wilf was concerned that they learn to give, hoping that soon they would be able to support a Latino pastor.

> Please pray (he wrote) about a *young latino pastor* for our church. We are 20 years older than the oldest in our congregation and 30 years older than the average. Younger men lead the services and serve as Superintendent of the Sunday School and on committees. They are wonderful, and, although we are busier and happier than we have ever been, we are not young any more.

Always looking to the mission fields, yet faithful to the task at hand, he continues in his letter with:

> We will not even give it consideration until our little church is adequately cared for, but we have *been invited to go to Bolivia, South America to do village work*. Florence's mission finds candidates to work in the urban areas. Although the cities are burgeoning, there remains a great need for workers in the "abandoned" villages of the hinterland.

Vancouver was a port of entry for immigrants from countries with political problems—Nicaragua, El Salvador, Chile.... A central hotel offered hospitality to these refugees until Canada could relocate them. These uprooted ones, some from communist regimes, others from anti-communist, a sprinkling of evangelicals amongst practicing and professing Catholics, were completely dependent on the Canadian government.

The Watsons and members of their congregation became concerned for these newcomers and regularly visited them, inviting them to meetings. An encouraging number showed interest and were chauffeured to the services. However, thousands were not being reached.

A Vancouver church sponsored "Hobbit House," a coffeehouse ministry. Graciously they offered Thursday nights for Latino Time to be sponsored by the Iglesia Evangélica. Enjoying refreshments at subsidized prices, multi-national Latinos entered for relaxation and socialization. Believers mingled with the guests, sitting with each small group of visitors, praying for opportunity to speak of their Lord. The Tirados joined this effort and were always thrilled to be able to speak for Jesus. The various nationality groups represented their countries with skits, effectively assisted by don Constantino, who had studied art and drama in Medellín.

"Don Wilfredo, let's visit that high-rise apartment complex. Refugees from many lands live there," suggested Constantino. "We can ring the bells next to Spanish names." Many refugees welcomed the Spanish-speakers, and many responded to the invitation to the Thursday night Latino Time at Hobbit House. Consequently several people found the Lord and joined the church.

To Everything There Is a Time   Ecclesiastes 3:1-8

As a boy, Wilfred had corresponded with his mother's godly father. Both were disappointed that they never met. Throughout his missionary career, limited finances prevented any thought of recreational travel. After the installation of the Argentine pastor in the Vancouver church, the Watsons eagerly responded to the invitation of Aunt Ida and his cousins to visit them in Yorkshire, England. In June of 1981, Wilf and Elizabeth flew from Vancouver to Toronto on the economy-class-no-frills Sky Bus and on to London. Cousins met them, entertained them in their homes, and escorted them to palaces, cathedrals, museums, and other tourist sites.

Visiting Aunt Ida in her hundredth year was the apex of the trip. In her, Wilfred saw and heard his dear mother who had died in a car accident during their Venezuelan experience; he loved her immediately. She still resided in the red brick, two story home of her youth. She enjoyed their Bible studies together, and daily trounced her guests in Scrabble.

The WEC International Headquarters castle near London was another thrill. "Their 65 acres were ablaze with color," he wrote. "The rhododendrons were at their best." Three staff meetings they were privileged to attend delighted them; he was asked at one of them to give the devotional message.

Entering the airport at the conclusion of their English vacation, the Watsons gave away all their British currency. They checked their luggage, passed security, watched the elderly and families with children board the plane—and then heard the announcement that because of a controllers' strike the plane would be delayed. No more flights that day! How they enjoyed the luxurious hotel and the scrumptious roast lamb with mint sauce, boiled new potatoes, garden peas and diced carrots. This was topped off with cherry pie and custard for "afters," all courtesy of the airline! But it was another story when they arrived in Toronto 20 hours late for their flight to Vancouver—with non-refundable excursion tickets. Because the delay was caused by British strikers, Air Canada arranged

for them to complete their trip a day late. "So," wrote Wilfred, "the vacation of a lifetime is over. Colossians 3:1-3."
Aunt Ida died before reaching her hundredth birthday. Wilf and Elizabeth were so glad they visited her when they did.

Vision Correctly Focused

Back in Vancouver, Wilfred resigned his pastorate, but not his church membership, on July 1, 1981, effective October first. Correspondence with Mr. Jim Davidson, field leader of SAM (the mission under which his daughter and son-in-law worked), brought a hearty invitation to return to Bolivia to do village work.

Excitement in anticipation of this second trip to Bolivia was mounting as he wrote to Florence and family a month before leaving Canada. He told of anticipated baptisms and reception of new members in their church, of renting their home to a ministerial student, of adequate regular income plus gifts for passage and outfit. ("What are the things you need?") He encouraged them to keep up Bible memorization with their little girls, to limit their dedication to ham radio, but to keep up their daily Bible reading and contact with the Lord, to pray together and with their co-workers. He told of a phone call from her brother Eric and his wife who were urging them to visit in Oklahoma en route to Miami.

The trip took a month, via the friends and relatives route, including a couple of days with Eric and Marge. In Miami their car license and insurance ran out. November 1, 1981 they parked their car at SAM's headquarters and flew to Bolivia.

After ten days of enjoying the Seatons in Santa Cruz, they proceeded 35 miles (56 km) east (an hour and a half by train) to the friendly village of Pailón, where a few believers gathered for Bible study and had commenced a church building, financed by mission funds. Foreign missionaries had visited regularly but had never resided there.

The Watsons were attracted to Pailón but *not* for physical reasons. The church, two blocks from the dusty main street, was 50 yards (45 m) from the tracks. However, trains fascinated Wilf and he appreciated the green grass and trees in between. Their granddaughters accompanied them for the initial week-end visit. It was hot!

The aqueduct, which normally functioned two hours in the morning and two in the evening, was out of order for ten days. The promise that it would be working on Sunday resulted in a cup of water in the morning and less in the evening. The thirsty little girls' pleas for water aggravated the grandparents' discomfort. A visit to an Indian village afforded baths and a gallon of water to take back to Pailón.

"But," wrote Wilfred, "if the *physical attractiveness* left much to be desired, the *spiritual attractiveness* more than compensated." In one month, attendance at Sunday services grew from 12 to 39 and the offerings from 47.50 bolivianos ($2) to over 200 bolivianos ($8).

Schoolteachers Walter and Aurora Aguilar were the only baptized members of the group. Within a few months several others, believers without previous opportunity for baptism, were prepared and immersed publicly in the Pailón creek.

Near the church, a 14 by 14 foot (4 by 4 m) construction of split palm stalks and a dirt floor provided their home at $20 per month. The Watsons purchased a length of double thickness plastic which could be split down the side and opened out to about six feet wide. This they laid out on the floor, securing it with their meager furniture. Perpetual guests felt comfortable sitting on the bed in a situation comparable to their own. The addition of a lean-to miniature kitchen doubled as the "master bedroom" while guests from Santa Cruz such as the Seaton five, who spent New Years with them, were offered the double bed in the livingroom-bedroom.

His monthly report to the SAM field leaders named members of his flock and told of their spiritual progress. He was dreaming of outreach from Pailón and anticipating the time when he could turn the work over to a Bolivian pastor.

In the fall of 1982 Wilfred wrote:

> Today is Canadian Thanksgiving Day and I am so thankful. "The lines are fallen unto me in pleasant places, yea I have a goodly heritage" (Psalm 16:6). We are thankful! Our work for the Lord has been a delight! We look forward to every activity in our little church that a year ago was a Sunday School class (10-15 people, adults and children) in a home.
>
> Now we have a little chapel, dirt floor, lacks one door, but all the ten benches are full and folks stand at the windows and listen. We have had baptisms twice this year and want to have more but the long cold dry season has dried up our creek just outside the village. If the warm spring breezes keep blowing, we will have rain soon and baptisms in late November. It will be a joy for us and for the dear ones who desire baptism.

In Perils of Robbers   *II Corinthians 11:26*

Most of their missionary career the Watsons were far from centers of civilization. But they made trips into the cities for mail, provisions, and visiting Florence, both when she was a child in boarding school in Colombia and later when she and her husband were missionaries in Bolivia.

Three months after establishing their home with the Guajibos in Colombia, the Watsons had driven the jeep up to Bogotá where they picked up their accumulated allowances. Elizabeth, savoring the joy of three months' mail, was occupying the jeep which was parked on the left-hand side of one of Bogotá's narrow, crowded, one-way streets while Wilf made some last-minute purchases. She was interrupted by a gentleman warning her, "Lady, some kids are trying to take the wheel off your jeep."

Sure enough, looking out the right side, there was the rogue, and Elizabeth yelled, "Skedaddle!"

The "gentleman" reached through the left window and grabbed her purse and disappeared. Gone was money for three months plus funds given especially for repairs for the jeep. She bounded out to chase him but he was gone. Wilf found her standing by the jeep, weeping.

"Sweetheart, what happened?"

"Oh, Wilf," she cried. "I fell for a trap. All our money is gone."

"Darling, sure, it'll hurt. But money is 'earthly things.' We are risen with Christ so we will 'seek those things which are above, where Christ sits on the right hand of God.' We're going to 'set (our) affections on things above, not on things on the earth.' "

Another time someone touched Elizabeth's arm and said, "You dropped something, Lady." Something had fallen from her purse and she wondered how it had happened. Looking at her purse she realized it was open—and her wallet was missing. Fortunately there was not nearly as much money, but there were important papers, including her driver's license. Again their life verse strengthened them. "They're only 'things on the earth.' " comforted Wilf. "We still have 'things above,' and they can't take them from us."

Even though the city in Bolivia was Santa Cruz (Holy Cross), that didn't suggest a holy nature. While living in Pailón, Pop and Mom Watson (as they were called by the SAM missionary family) frequently took the morning train into town, for the day. In his March 1982 letter he wrote:

Col. 3:1-3. "...Seek things that are above. Set your affections on things above." You know this is our life's verse. We thought we knew a little about its truth. We wish we were so "other worldly minded" we really could "take *joyfully* the spoiling of our (earthly) goods" (Heb. 10:34). But we are so slow to learn.

Florence drove Elizabeth to town where they bought a few items which they locked in the car with Elizabeth's purse hidden under the seat. While they proceeded with their errands a thief pried open the door and took it all. More important than the $50 in the purse were her license and other papers. But here was the "knockout blow." We had borrowed David's foolproof camera and had taken two rolls of colored slides to take home to show you in August. *They were all taken with the purse.* We were so pleased with them, and half an hour after receiving them, they were stolen. We put an ad in the paper but nothing has shown up. We were crushed by this loss, but knew the Lord was speaking to our hardened old hearts.

The Windows of Heaven Opened   *II Kings 7*

Three days after the thievery, their visas, due to expire in August 1982, were extended to January 1984. Since they had established residence in Canada and were each receiving Canadian pensions, they decided Elizabeth should become a Canadian citizen. In the process, her time out of Canada was limited. The normal six-month period had already been extended to a year because they were in nonremunerative missionary work. If she didn't return, her $200 per month would be endangered. Besides the Canadian pension, they had USA Social Security, plus continuing support from churches and individuals. Their March 1982 letter continued:

> We felt the Lord was saying to us, "Can you trust Me, without the help of the Canadian government and stay where you are needed?" But $2400 was more than either of us had received in any year we were on the mission field.
>
> We thought, "The world is facing great inflation! We can't forfeit that money which the Lord has provided for us!" Well, we are going to stay here for as long as we are needed, even *for the duration* ... and we are excited about staying.

Don't feel sorry for us or think that we are short. We are not. Without our missionary faith promise pledge we could live on $100 a month here in Bolivia. No car, no T.V., no radio, no utility bills (there are no utilities), no ice cream, no shopping centers, but we do have nice fresh vegetables and fruit and pay little for our two room shack. We would rather be penalized $200 a month and stay working here than receive it and go home and do nothing. So we are staying here.

Do not send us money. It gets stolen. We are not short a bit and doubt we will be even if we lose the pension. If we need it or God wants us to have it, He will work on the Canadian government to continue giving it to us.

Pray for the Seatons, our kids working in Santa Cruz. Living costs there, especially education, are unreal. Folks want to help us old codgers, but the young folks have a rough time. Our kids have one of the cheapest missionary homes in Santa Cruz and pay $250 a month (American). They have to move in June and comparable houses cost $350-$450 a month.

Your very happy missionary friends in Bolivia,
Wilf and Elizabeth Watson

September of that year (1982) they were both scheduled to lose their pensions. The law stated: "Pensioners who have less than 20 years residence in Canada after age 18 will be paid for the month of departure and six months more. Payment will then be suspended until it has been established that they have returned to reside in Canada again." Wilf's reaction was:

We *never* paid taxes in Canada and felt unworthy of the pension so never thought of begging for it since we had disqualified ourselves. We *did* thank them for the money we had received those three years. We told them we were doing unremunerated missionary work and felt the Lord wanted us to stay here even if we did lose the pension that had been a blessing to us. We never asked anyone to pray that "the law of the Medes and Persians, that changeth not" should make a concession for us. They had already made one concession in giving it to us for a *year* instead of the legal six months after we left Canada. In November we received a letter saying *we could stay here in missionary work for as long as we wished* and the pension would be deposited in our bank account and that the two months lost would be repaid!!!

Can't you see what a thrill it is to serve the Lord??? We *did* receive some *special Christmas gifts* that we feel came because you thought we might be short of money. We will return them unless we are authorized to use them for needy Bolivian coworkers. They surely could use the help.

We will be returning to Canada in early September to retain Elizabeth's immigrant status in Canada. Wilf is Canadian and has no legal right to *live* in the States now. Elizabeth is American and will lose *her* right to *live* in Canada after September 15. With the two years we have been in Bolivia (and they *do* count), she will now have five years residence in Canada and can get Canadian citizenship. We are going home to do that. We don't want to get separated at this stage of our marriage. If young folks only knew how important marriage can be at our age they would work harder at it.

I have no grievance with the USA that has been so good to me, first in giving me a wife and also supporting me on the mission field for 45 years, but it might be beneficial here to be Canadian rather than American. Bolivia borrowed more than $8 billion from the USA during 20 years of rotten corrupt military governments that squandered it on themselves and useless projects. Now payday has come and Bolivia finds itself enslaved to a bitterly hated Uncle Sam from whom she would like emancipation.

As soon as legal affairs are taken care of we intend to return to Bolivia. Both the Bolivians and the missionaries are pressing us for a promise to return. Bless them! They are all precious!

It Is the Lord That Heals   *Exodus 15:26*

Quiet and privacy were generally available in the Pailón church where Wilf was wont to study his Bible. The doors and windows were closed to keep out the heat. One morning the main door squeaked, opened, and admitted an immaculately dressed diminutive Indian gentleman. Wilf sized up the well-proportioned stranger: five feet tall with tiny hands, tiny feet, all fine features and judged him to be half his own size—less than 100 pounds (45 kg) and 50 years of age. He wore a white starched shirt and an attractive tie. His well-pressed blue serge pants looked like the edge of a knife. His shoes would pass military inspection.

Wilf looked into his face. His jet black hair and small mustache were perfectly groomed in western style; his eyes pleaded for help. "Are you the pastor here? Can you help me?"

"I'm at your orders, Sir. What is your problem?"

"I'm the town drunk. I'm a public school teacher." Making a sweep of his arms from the east straight up over his head, he continued, "Every morning I could be found in front of my class in the schoolhouse." Then sweeping his other hand from the noon position straight down towards the west he continued, "And in the afternoons anyone could find me at my favorite drinking joint or outside lying in the gutter, drunk. Because of my excessive drinking, I have contracted tuberculosis. I have just returned after six months in a TB sanitorium, declared incurable. Everybody knows I have TB. The schoolboard is about to fire me: my disease is contagious, the children are susceptible and I would be a menace. I've been teaching for thirty years and I can't do anything else."

"Well, don Carmelo," (his name was Carmelo Escobar) "I can't help you but I know Someone who can. You have a problem far worse than your drinking habit and far worse than your tuberculosis. Your biggest problem is your sin. It will lead you to a Christless eternity and condemnation in an eternal hell. That is the first problem to consider. Ask the Lord Jesus to forgive your sins and to come into your heart. Trust in Him as your only Savior."

Down they knelt on the dirt floor. Pastor Wilfredo prayed a simple prayer and Mr. Escobar repeated it phrase by phrase.

"Don Carmelo, you have taken care of the most important problem: the salvation of your soul. I'm going to pray that the Lord will deliver you from your drink habit, and that He will heal you of your tuberculosis."

Standing up and placing his hand on the shoulder of his new brother, the pastor prayed, "Oh, God, I'm not a healing evangelist. I don't pretend to have the gift of healing, but I believe You will answer prayer. You have told us that if we ask anything in Your name, You will do it. So, in Jesus' name, I ask You to give this man complete victory over this habit that has dominated him for more than half his life. And, Lord Jesus, I pray that You will heal him of tuberculosis, completely and instantaneously, in a way that will bring honor and glory to You and be a testimony to the power of the Lord Jesus Christ. I pray in Jesus' name, amen."

"Don Carmelo, take the six-thirty Santa Cruz train tomorrow morning. Ask the doctor for a chest x-ray and for a certificate of the findings."

Wilfred spent the entire next day in prayer and fasting. The daily train returned at seven o'clock that evening. Mr. Escobar sprinted to the parsonage, waving a piece of paper and bubbling with good news. "Pastor Wilfredo, I did as you told me and had a chest x-ray. The doctor gave me a certificate showing that I have absolutely no sign of anything on my lungs!" Nearly exploding with joy, he thrust a paper into the pastor's hand. "Here's the certificate that I am free from tuberculosis!"

Praising the Lord for His healing, Wilf told the teacher, "Have copies made and take one to the school board and another to the teachers' union which will have to defend you; there are now no grounds for firing you."

Mr. Escobar was jumping for joy and together the two men thanked the Lord for healing his body. The pastor prayed again, this time for complete victory over the terrible habit of alcohol which had dominated his life for so long. Again God answered prayer, and Carmelo Escobar was completely delivered.

Early one Sunday morning several weeks later, don Carmelo quietly entered the church and took his accustomed place in the third bench from the front. He frequently arrived early for fellowship with his pastor. This morning he opened up a subject dear to his heart. "Brother Wilfredo, I want to be baptized."

"Brother Carmelo, everybody in town knows that you have been living with that woman for thirty years. If I baptized you without being married, everybody would say, 'Huh, look at those evangelicals. They live exactly like everyone else. There's no difference. Why should I become an evangelical?'

"None of the evangelical churches in all Latin America would approve your baptism. But, Brother Carmelo, you don't need baptism to be saved. You are as saved as any person who has been baptized. There is not enough water in this world to make you any cleaner than you've already been made by the blood of Jesus Christ. It's only the blood of Jesus Christ that cleanses us from all sin. You have trusted in that blood and you're just as much saved as I am, just as much as the thief on the cross who was never baptized, but Jesus said, 'Today you will be with me in Paradise.' Until you see your way clear to marry your woman, we can't baptize you."

"I'll never marry that witch," and he began describing her violent temper. The neighbors trembled when that bitter, aggressive woman cursed and swore in both Spanish and Quechua.

Regular as clockwork, every Sunday he would plead, "Please! My baptism, my baptism!" and the answer was consistent: "I'm sorry. I can't baptize you."

Came the day when the diminutive Indian brought his corpulent woman to the parsonage, both dressed their best. "Brother Wilfredo, we're ready to get married. Come with us." Joyously Wilfred and Elizabeth dropped all activities and plans to accompany their friends for their civil ceremony. The four then went to the Escobar home where they put together some lemonade and the pastor prayed over their marriage union.

On Easter Sunday, a year after his salvation, don Carmelo joyfully entered the waters of baptism, and in June of that year his wife, having attended church regularly and having accepted the Lord as her Savior, followed him. The neighbors were amazed at the change in this truly converted woman.

Wilfred was sometimes asked what he did socially for the desperately poor Bolivians. He was tempted to say, "Almost nothing." But then he would think of schoolteacher Escobar who had been earning $30 per month plus medical insurance and retirement pension. Most of that pittance would go for liquor, leaving him with $5 to $10. Naturally his woman was angry. But Wilf taught this new eager believer the blessing of tithing. Rather than impoverishing him, his new life of godly stewardship netted him $27 per month. They bought an addition to their home. They bought a stereo tape recorder. Every time Wilf visited them he noticed something new and attractive. "Social programs," said Wilf, "tend to work from the outside in. God's program changes the heart and works from the inside out and it's infinitely more effective and infinitely more economical than any other social program." Don Carmello was a hilarious giver and whenever any work was to be done on the church, he was the first to give a generous offering above his tithe.

One of Wilf's illustrations, reported by Bolivian pastor Luis Bravo, was of the Christian who had a coin in his pocket. On the coin was the likeness of a llama, Bolivian beast of burden. At the time of the offering, the man held that coin so tightly in his pocket that the poor llama began to bleat. So he pulled the money out and, although it hurt him to give it, he deposited it in the offering plate.

Hindrance Brings Increase

A teacher in the local school frequently visited the Watsons and asked Wilf to help him teach English. The priest who taught religion there influenced the principal to expel the foreigner, but the teacher and

116   *Church Planting and Development:*

"The blood of Jesus Christ cleanses us from all sin."

students interceded and Wilf returned. The priest retaliated with a procession, bringing a huge image into the Watsons' yard. Paraders peeked through the window to catch reactions. Since the priest forbade attendance at the evangelical services, many people began standing around the windows listening; the more courageous ones entered.

Within 20 months the church had grown from one Bolivian couple to 18 baptized members, plus Wilf and Elizabeth. The ten benches were filled at most services, the windows crowded with listeners. Several of the teenagers were preparing for baptism prior to the Watsons' August departure. The congregation was ready for a Bolivian pastor.

Biking to Paradise

Pailón was not Wilf's only parish. A member, Julio, claimed a homestead 36 miles (58 km) out in the jungle, in a place called Paraíso (Paradise). He returned to Pailón with reports of the scattered homesteaders to whom he had witnessed. Several had been saved; others were open to the gospel. He invited Wilf to accompany him on his return trip. Julio had an old bike and Wilf, a new one. Together they pedaled, pushed, and carried those bikes over a miserable excuse for a road. At times the swamp extended for almost half a mile, but the two kept going. For three days they ministered to the poverty-stricken converts. Others joined the group. The return trip was just as taxing.

In spite of Elizabeth's protestations, six weeks later the 67-year-old biker felt constrained to return, so repeated the ordeal alone. Homes were sometimes as far as 15 miles apart on this little-used trail. Wilf was glad to visit those few homes to rest and witness to the love of Jesus.

Arriving at Paraíso, he rejoiced to see Julio and his group maturing in their Christian life. He repeated the trip several times.

In dry season after the road was completed, SAM missionary John DePue drove Wilf and Jeff Jenkins, his guest from Memphis, to Paraíso for several days of meetings.

"Everybody was awaiting a visit from Wilf [related Mr. DePue]. We walked several kilometers visiting the scattered homes. It was amazing to see how many of the people eagerly anticipated Wilf's visit and his sharing God's Word."

Wilf's heart went out to these "dear folks. They live like animals in huts made of frames with plastic coverings. Both nights *everyone* in the colony walked in the dark to come to the service." The lack of diversion in the community encouraged total participation. Of course, Wilf had previously visited them all and they were captivated by his loving concern for them. His accordion and singing would announce the time of service.

Traveling without Class

The daily commuter train into Santa Cruz resembled a schoolbus on train tracks; other trips involved boxcars or flatcars without seats, all dreadfully overcrowded. One could purchase a second-class ticket to ride in the passenger coach, with slim chance of squeezing on. The flatcars had the advantage of fresh air blowing over the odors of raw meat, baskets of live chickens, and jungle fruits and vegetables for market combined with unwashed bodies—with *no* sanitary facilities in any part of the train. None of the cars offered space to stretch or move about.

In March 1983 Wilf and Augusto Chávez from Santa Cruz, a layman with a gift of evangelism, took the first jam-packed freight train after a railroad strike east toward Brazil to Fortín Suárez Arana. Arriving at the fort, Wilf with his small accordion and Augusto with his guitar attracted soldiers from the barracks (several asked for prayer) and preached also in the church.

"The three services in the church grew in attendance," reported Wilf. "The final night, every available seat was filled and folks were standing. Too bad we had to leave just as we were getting real momentum."

Northeast to the Santiago Sierra they proceeded several hours by train to Roboré. Two small services in a home seemed to be attended by all Christians and Wilf was "tempted not to give an evangelistic message, but that was the idea of the tour so I did preach to unsaved. One man was saved in the service."

All Wednesday night they slept on the floor of the crowded swaying train to Chochís where they had five services. Several people asked for prayer for salvation.

Sunday afternoon the daily train took them to San José de Chiquitos. The ancient, rusted-out, coaches where travelers filled every inch of aisles and between broken-down seats, offered little improvement over the boxcars. Wilf nudged a place where he could sleep between passengers wrapped in their filthy blankets surrounded by their bundles, sacks, and produce.

At San José they spent their longest time—a full week. There they received the only offering of the trip. "I gave mine to brother Chávez," wrote Wilf in his report to the SAM office. "I also gave him a little gift from my own money. He needs help badly. He prayed for his two sons who need tennis shoes for gym class, so he was glad he could buy those and a few other necessities."

Wilf concluded his report to the mission with, "This is the longest either of us has been away from his wife for years. But the glorious results for eternity justified our sacrifice and the sacrifice of those who attended night after night."

Dynamic Teaching at CCC

A special two-year school for men with families, called the *Centro de Capacitación Cristiana* (CCC or Christian Training Center) was established in a rural area in 1982. Eight men, most with families, were accepted each year. After the first year, the two classes studied together. One missionary couple served as directors and deans. Missionary and Bolivian teachers rotated, each being assigned a two-week course. The men studied mornings while their wives cared for the babies and cooked. Afternoons, the wives were in class and the men did assigned chores. The children attended the local public school which required uniforms and school supplies—all paid for by the mission.

Dynamic teachers being needed for the initial learning experience at the leadership training center, Wilf and Elizabeth were chosen. Wilf taught "Encounters with Christ," to the men. Other times he taught the Gospel of John and the Acts of the Apostles. Elizabeth taught literacy, child evangelism, and homemaking to the wives. The Watsons were thrilled to be able to take Julio and Eulalia Arandia with two small children from Pailón to the school.

"They fulfilled all of our expectations and more," wrote the founding director, Gary Lengkeek, of the senior teachers.

> Having Wilf and Elizabeth living with us those first two traumatic weeks will always be a special memory to us [continued Mr. Lengkeek]. They encouraged constantly. They supported our objectives. They were excited about the prospects of the program. They taught in each trimester they were in Bolivia if they had no interfering commitments.

It wasn't only the Watsons who enjoyed the two-week stints at the Bible school. So did the students, the resident missionaries, and the children. Old bald Wilf made a joke of pleading for a hair cut. "There's nothing to cut," remonstrated the student barber. "That bit of hair around the edges is so fine—I've never seen such fine hair."

Cecilia Ramsey, wife of a successor director at CCC confessed:

I often neglected my four small children for the ministry. Sometimes they just ran around outside and played. At times we had 45-50 children and every afternoon when the women were in class you'd see Pop out there sitting in a chair, with two or three in his lap and he'd be telling Bible stories. Many times he'd select a story book from my house and then gather my little ones on his lap and read to them. "More, Pop! More, Pop! More, more!" I'd hear them squeal. They just loved to see him come. He amazed me! Many people wouldn't pick up the Bolivian kids or even mine, because they ran around dirty and their noses would be runny. Yet it didn't seem to bother Pop. I always loved to have him come. My kids would scream, "Here comes Grandpa! Here comes Grandpa!"

Christ Is Magnified   *Philippians 1:20*

In his letter to his beloved Lem Fowler which he signed, "Your Timothy," Wilf told about speaking to 35 señoritas and 5 fellows, all Evangelical University nursing students, at a weekend outing. Upon arrival, he learned he was to speak twice instead of just once, so, leaving his prepared message for later:

I told how a young man with jet black hair, like they all had, took interest in a no-good street urchin and led him to the Lord and "discipled" him for the next 59 years. I told them my age, 69 years old yesterday.

That afternoon I gave my prepared message from Philippians 1:20: "According to my earnest expectation and my hope, that in nothing I shall be ashamed, but that with all boldness, as always, so now also Christ shall be magnified in my body, whether by life, or by death."

Magnifying Christ:

1. Manner of this Magnification: Magnify Him before a world that does not appreciate Him (John 1:10).

2. Means of the magnification: in my body (Romans 12:1). God has no body, so needs ours to display Himself to the unbelieving world that does not know Him. Satan has no body and wants ours and often gets it.

3. Measurement of the magnification: As always, so now. Importance of good habits.
Thought is mother of the deed;

Deed is mother of the habit;
Habit is mother of character;
Character is mother of destiny.
We will be what we are becoming.

4. Motive of magnification: Not magnifying ourselves or drawing attention to ourselves, but helping others.

SAM capitalized on Wilf's gifts and asked him to conduct evangelistic campaigns in all the churches of the mission, and to preach twice at their national convention. Then the Baptists asked him to do the same at their convention.

In April 1983, his son-in-law David Seaton flew him and Augusto Chávez far east to Indian country. His report on that trip mentioned 14 places where they ministered.

Two weeks of teaching at CCC were squeezed in, and then June 27th, Pilot Kemper flew Wilf, Elizabeth, and their visitor, Jeff, to Sandoval near the Brazilian border for concentrated Bible teaching and evangelistic meetings.

It was the highlight of a most exciting two years in Bolivia [wrote Wilf]. The pilot shuttled five or six people, (depending on size) from six villages to our central location. We slept, taught, and ate in the schoolhouse with 75 new Christians or unsaved folks. We taught them the Bible before and after breakfast, and each afternoon. We had nightly evangelistic services. At least a dozen made profession of faith and the Christians were just bubbling over, enjoying the fellowship, the Bible study, and the food we had brought. Souls were saved and Christians edified and we, too, were ministered unto by the grateful folks. They were five absolutely glorious days.

Between August 8-13 they made a quick visit to four churches on the railroad for farewells. On the 14th, baptisms and the Lord's Supper were held in Pailón. August 19th they left Santa Cruz for Miami and continued to Canada to establish Elizabeth's residency and a year of traveling, visiting, and, of course, preaching!

Wilf's July 1983 report to the mission reads:

We are grateful to the South America Mission for allowing us to serve the Lord these last two years in South America. We are all too conscious that folks our age can get in the way of younger

·missionaries and be more bother than they are worth. We are very grateful to you folks and assure you we will use our return tickets in January 1984 if you will let us. We may want to go home again in August 1984 for four months but will return, Lord willing, for at least two or three years. So we would suggest an itinerant ministry, but will do whatever you feel we could do and where we would be most useful.

Good News from Bolivia   *Proverbs 25:25*

While in Vancouver that winter, they were thrilled to hear that their beloved church in Pailón was thriving. They had installed as pastor Julio Arandia who, with Eulalia and their five little ones had recently completed their two-year course at CCC.

SAM requested the Watsons to locate in the far eastern city of San José, a larger city than Pailón, situated at the mid-point between Santa Cruz and the Brazilian border. "We will work under the fine older Bolivian pastor whom I know and love greatly," wrote 70-year-old Wilfred. The 60-year-old pastor had graduated from Bible School in San José, then taught there until it disbanded. After that, he combined pastoring, which was his labor of love, with high school teaching, and fine leatherwork and engravings on paper and leather in order to help his many children attend university. He had a strong conviction against taking any money from his church because of the limited finances of the members. Although he was a top-notch Bible teacher and preacher and a much sought-after evangelist and camp speaker, and was highly respected in his community as an intellectual and spiritual giant, the work was suffering and needed a "shot in the arm. Pray that we can be a spark in God's hand," wrote Wilf, "for that needy pastor and town." No missionaries within 100 miles in any direction would allow for "lots of elbow room."

Daughter Florence wrote that David had been loaned to the New Tribes Mission to help in their flying program in chilly Cochabamba, 8000 feet (2438 m) high, and 200 air miles (320 km) from Santa Cruz. The Seatons were thrilled with their new assignment.

Relatives, Citizenship, and Travel

After a fruitful and enjoyable stay in Vancouver, rejoicing in the growth of their church, the Watsons flew to California to visit Elizabeth's family and church, and then on to Texas for a week with Eric and his wife, Marge. Dad wrote to Florence:

Eric bought a $75,000 Freightliner Truck Tractor in mid November with which he pulls trailers on contract. He and Marge work together, taking turns driving and sleeping. They haul chemicals 1000 miles [1600 km] from Houston to north of Pittsburgh. It's hard work but both are making truckdrivers' pay. They logged 50,000 miles [80,000 km] in three months, so he took it for a check-up on the warranty. The truck was in the shop that week, so we had a glorious time together.

Returning to Vancouver the Watsons rented a small apartment for three months (their home was rented out) and delighted in escorting visiting English cousins over 3000 miles [4800 km] by land and 1000 (1600) by sea-ferry, during a month of Canadian sight-seeing.

On her birthday, May 23, 1984, Elizabeth was sworn in as a Canadian. Two days later she received a Canadian passport and on May 26th the expedition back to Bolivia began. Through western Canada and the States they drove their mini station wagon, visiting along the way and reaching SAM headquarters in Lake Worth, Florida a month later.

There they met ten Bible college students whom they escorted to Colombia for six weeks of physical and spiritual ministry with WEC. The team participated in evangelism and construction of a Bogotá church and a Bible camp in the eastern jungles, beyond Villavicencio. The Watsons had the joy of meeting "so many dear old friends. It was a thrilling experience. We spoke in many churches and were most gratified with the results."

Sitting Where They Sat *Ezekiel 3:15*

August 15, 1984 the team flew to Miami. The exhausted young people returned to WEC headquarters at Camp Hill for debriefing while the crisp seniors reported to the SAM office and proceeded to Bolivia before their round-trip tickets expired August 20th. The all-night flight landed in Santa Cruz at 8:00 A.M. Eager to visit the dearly-loved church which they had left a year before, they boarded the next train to Pailón for a brief visit.

Two hundred miles (320 km) west from Santa Cruz flew the grandparents to Cochabamba for a few days with the Seaton five. "It was a thrill to be with them," wrote Grandpa after the eastward trip of 400 miles (640 km). "But we were glad to arrive in San José de Chiquitos." (St. Joseph of the small people, considering the diminutive size of the local Indians.)

An earlier letter to Pastor Luis Bravo had asked for help in finding a residence for them. "Don't consider us as being Americans or millionaires; if it's good enough for Bolivians it will be good enough for us." The only place available were two Sunday School rooms with a large corridor behind the church. Running water meant running to Bravo's tile-roofed adobe home next door with a bucket. They were invited to share the Bravos' "shower" (a boarded-in enclosure with a dipper). Probably all eleven children were not home at once. Big luxury was an outhouse in the back yard. During the two months they waited for their household equipment to arrive, they accepted the gracious hospitality of the Bravo family. Wilf's concern was:

> that we be at our best for the Lord. It is not what we *have* that will determine how much we do for God but what we *are*. It is not the quality of the *outfit* that we take to the mission field but the quality of the *infit*. Paul, my missionary ideal, was "poor yet making many rich" (II Cor. 6:10).

In January he had discussed in a letter why he didn't want a new pickup truck and be "the rich gringo" in a town where the wealthiest few had vehicles from the '60s, or a motorcycle "that would put a material wall between us and the folks who earn a dollar a day when they can get work." Even a new bicycle "would set us off from those who are thrilled to have one that is held together with bailing wire."

In 1992 Pastor Luis Bravo wrote that he had worked with many missionaries and named three prominent men whom he admired greatly.

> But, [he wrote], I always admired my brother Wilfredo, for his valor and dedication to the work, even though he was older than the rest of us. Every morning after breakfast and again at about two o'clock he went out to visit the church members. During his year-and-a-half with us, we saw the church enlivened. He visited all around San José, at times by foot, other times by train, which was distressingly uncomfortable, but the ruggedness of the ride didn't bother him. He was willing to ride in any available space.

> Once they were traveling northwest to Concepción [CCC] for the two week stint at the training center. Rather than going by train to Santa Cruz and then flying 200 miles to Concepción the Watsons left at dawn for the military toll gate to wait for a vehicle going north toward San Ignacio. As luck would have it, nothing was going

that way. Finally, towards sundown, a logging truck pulled in which was going in that direction, and they climbed aboard with their luggage. In the middle of the night, at a deserted place, the driver put them off. They tried to bed down but the plague of mosquitoes prevented sleep. Before dawn they heard cocks crowing and figured they must be near a habitation. But these predicaments didn't discourage them since this type of experience happened repeatedly.

The Watsons continued their trek to Concepción by whatever vehicles the Lord sent their way.

They didn't need much furniture to keep up with their neighbors. A crate served for a typing chair; a board bed with a thin foam-rubber mattress would be given to guests while the hosts slept on sleeping bags in the office/kitchen; benches borrowed from the church accommodated visitors, including a Sunday School class. They did have a radio, a tape recorder, typewriter, minimal kitchen equipment, etc. that they had brought with them on the ten-hour freight train trip from Santa Cruz.

Upon returning from visitation one night that first month, they realized their home had been burglarized—the radio, tape recorder, and other things were missing. They tightened the security, but two weeks later at a repeat performance the replacement radio and other things disappeared. Double locks on the door and bars on the windows of the kitchen/office where the more valuable items were used and kept seemed to solve the problem.

Over half the congregation lived a kilometer south on the edge of town so every Wednesday Wilf and Elizabeth would walk over that way, visit their homes, receive a snack and coffee, then have Bible study and prayer with them. The thieves obviously knew their schedule and took advantage of their evenings out.

The corridor of the Watsons' home served as diningroom/parlor to which a supply of table games attracted the young people. When Wilf visited towns along the railroad, Elizabeth generally stayed home and entertained the youth, who, in turn, kept her company.

Pitifully few parishioners participated in the church services. Pastor Bravo, a truly excellent Bible teacher, had not encouraged others to share the responsibilities. Wilf, the oldest man in the church, was entrusted with the Young People's class, which met in that corridor. It grew to 35 members. He stimulated the congregation, especially his young people's class, to participate.

Fellow-missionary, Tim Ramsey, visited that hot, humid city. Wilf invited the younger man to accompany him to Villa Fátima several miles away. Witnessing door to door, they were welcomed into a home. Wilf opened his Bible to Philippians 3:7-11 and talked about Paul, who had given up all for Christ. "Clearly," said Mr. Ramsey, "this man could honestly share these scriptures, because he, as Paul, had really given up all, had sacrificed much for the name of Jesus."

Transportational options west to Santa Cruz for the monthly trips for mail, supplies, a phone call to Florence in Cochabamba, and mission activities, such as the quarterly two-week session at CCC were: all night scrunched on the floor of the crowded passenger train, or finding a bit more space on the floor of a flat car for eight hours of rain or sun with a multitude of Bolivians.

Going east to the Brazilian border the Watsons chose the flatcar, and for ten hours they huddled en route to a pastorless congregation. What joy they had ministering to those needy believers! From midnight to midmorning, returning west, they repeated the ordeal a week later.

"It's good to be home," sighed Wilf to Elizabeth as they walked the two blocks from the railroad.

"Wilf, there's Pastor Bravo." She sensed something was amiss.

"Brother Wilfredo," lamented this humble, honest man. "You've been robbed again. The door is broken. Here's your clock and some other things I found in my house."

The heavy-hearted father, who dearly loved the Watsons but was unable to control his children, walked away. The weary Watsons appraised the situation. Besides the lock and door that would have to be replaced, many other things were missing. All concerned knew the thief was from the Bravo household, but Wilf chose to "take joyfully the spoiling of their goods" and cling again to his life verse, Colossians 3:1-3, setting his affections on things above rather than on typewriters, watches, and sleeping bags.

Within six months, church attendance was up to 90 on a Sunday evening. After one year in San José, Wilf reported:

The little church has grown: four new families have entered the fellowship; several believers were baptized at each of two baptismal services and more are in preparation; four new preaching centers have been opened in surrounding areas. The previously discouraged pastor is now rejoicing.

Before long the Watsons understood the reasons for the anemic condition in which they had found the church. Besides the thievery within the pastor's household, the pastor and his seven eldest children had all either engendered or conceived prior to marriage. The pastor told Wilf, "Premarital sex isn't adultery; extra-marital sex is." He had filtered his interpretation of scripture through the local culture, but he was obviously faithful to his wife throughout their long marriage.

Grace Cubas, an American missionary married to a Peruvian missionary, was impressed with the Watsons' "humility and courage in kindly and tactfully confronting sin, standing up for scriptural principles and practice."

The electric plant in San José functioned for four hours each evening. Unexpectedly the lights failed while Elizabeth was out disposing of garbage. Stumbling back to the house in the pitch darkness, she fell against a wall and injured her shoulder. The local "doctor's" examination produced the diagnosis, "No break. No dislocation. Just badly bruised. Take pain pills."

Two days later, in great pain, she returned for the same diagnosis. (The "doctor" needed to stand by his diagnosis to save face.) With ointment and pills she tried to keep comfortable and thought, "I must be pretty much of a sissy if I can't take a bad bruise." Two weeks later the diagnosis was the same.

United with her husband in dedication to a commitment, Elizabeth would not be deterred by a bruised shoulder and accompanied him to a planned four-day evangelistic campaign on the Brazilian border. Ten hours on Monday they chugged along, seated on the floor of a crowded boxcar, Wilf providing a human backrest for his wife. God blessed and at least one family's life was changed by the power of the gospel.

Saturday the ten-hour ordeal was repeated. The pain in Elizabeth's shoulder intensified. On Sunday, Wilf taught his young people's class and preached the evening sermon, after which they selected the crowded passenger train for a night of jostling into Santa Cruz. Elizabeth was given a seat and Wilf slept on the floor at her feet. To the doctor they went.

"What does the X ray show, Doctor?"

"That shoulder is out five centimeters [2 in]. When did this injury occur?"

"Almost three weeks ago."

"I've never set a shoulder that long out of joint, without surgery; but I'll see what I can do." He pushed it into place and applied a cast which provided some comfort. The rugged pioneers returned to San José.

Three weeks later another trip to town was required to remove the cast. Then back to San José! Two days after that ten-hour jogging, the shoulder slipped out again. Third trip to Santa Cruz—this time for surgery! "Señora Watson, a tendon across your arm that should be four centimeters [1½ in] was over five centimeters [2 in]. I had to cut it and tie your bone in place." He put on another cast. "Stay in the city for awhile. I want to see if you can move your hand or wrist."

After two weeks in town and two weeks teaching at the CCC they returned to the doctor who advised, "You need at least two weeks of physical therapy. Do the best you can, but never expect normal use of your shoulder. You may be able to use your hand, wrist, and elbow; but you'll never be able to raise your hand above your head. I'll drive you to the therapist."

In the car the doctor began reviewing his relations with the Watsons. "Remember, you gave me a New Testament and marked the Gospel of John. I began reading it. You gave me a business card and an invitation to a professional men's Bible study. I began attending, and it has been a great blessing. I took my wife to one of their retreats. It was great! This spring I'm going to the States for three reasons: first, I know a little English and I want to use it; second, I want to see the orthopedic sections in your hospitals and learn what they're doing; third, I want time to read my Bible."

"Glory, hallelujah!" came from both Wilfred and Elizabeth, who later reported, "It was worth my three months of aches and pains to get this contact with that doctor."

They returned to San José for a final three months. Diligently stretching her arm, pulling down the clothes line, and clipping clothes pins, Elizabeth experienced progress.

A dear friend wrote to her, "Elizabeth, the Scriptures are full of admonitions to lift holy hands in praise and prayer to the Lord. Sister, lift them up." And lift them she did as the Lord strengthened her arms. The present writer heard her give this testimony six months later and saw her raise her hands all the way up—as good as new!

Easter week of 1986 climaxed their year-and-a-half of fruitful service in San José. Tim and Cecilia Ramsey visited and joined in the dedication of a new deacon and elder to the church board. Eleven believers were baptized in a swimming pool about three miles (5 km) out of town on Palm Sunday. The members rejoiced in their new life and in the good ministry of an assistant pastor, a recent graduate of the CCC. From Thursday to Sunday night all benches were filled as they celebrated the death and resurrection of our Lord. A "first" for the Watsons was the certificate of gratitude, crafted by Pastor Bravo, which the church awarded them for 18 months of service.

Their Bolivian brothers remember the sermons don Wilfredo preached and the Sunday School lessons he taught. They remembered his little messages in their homes and his ministry of encouragement. They saw and remembered how Elizabeth helped Wilfred to be a better missionary (they didn't know about her pre-engagement prayer, "Lord, it's not for personal reasons that I want to get married. But if I could help him to be a better missionary, I would be glad to say, 'Yes'"), how she was always ready to help her husband as well as any of them. But most of all they remembered that they sat where the common people sat—as had Ezekiel with the poor Israelite captives by the River Chebar.

Following the Easter services, the Watsons and Ramseys elbowed their way onto the night train through a crowd of protesting passengers who shouted, "There's not room for one more." A young Christian—whom Joe Kemper was teaching to become a mission pilot—saw them, and he and his friend gave Elizabeth and Cecilia their seats for the all-night trip to Santa Cruz; Tim and Wilf were cramped on the filthy floor between seats or in the aisle. This time Wilfred and Elizabeth were en route to the United States and Canada.

Continuing Challenges for the Septuagenarians

During seven months in North America, the Watsons covered 22,000 miles (35,200 km) with not so much as a flat tire. November 7, 1986 they left Miami for their fourth night-flight to Santa Cruz.

As before, they made themselves available for assignment. For eight years SAM missionaries had watched their adopted Pop and Mom set an example of courage, humility, sacrifice, love, and commitment to Jesus Christ. SAM missionary John DePue reported,

> It wasn't right that at his age he should be running up and down the railroad, climbing on and off flat cars, and enduring so much hardship. He wouldn't limit himself so we limited him by assigning him to teach in Santa Cruz in a seminary which had 120 students, including some SAM students. There he had a tremendous ministry.

Pop was assigned six to ten class hours and Mom corrected correspondence courses for over 50 students, in spite of both of them struggling with cataracts not yet ripe for surgery. By May 1987 Wilf was finding it difficult to use reference works and to read the students' papers. Quarterly "vacations" involved a two hundred mile (320 km) flight north for their two-week stint at the CCC.

Eager to return to church planting, Wilf pestered Mr. DePue, "John, when are we going to canvas the shantytowns for a church site? The Lord has already provided money to buy a lot and build a church with some rooms for us."

"Pop, you have an apartment by the seminary. You have electricity and hot and cold running water and a phone. Why can't you be content there?"

"I want to live with the people."

Villa Bolivia, one of many shantytowns, presented a challenging need. No church of any kind was located in the 36 square blocks. Three thousand new inhabitants had assembled homes there from cartons, flattened tin cans, pieces of wood, and building material scavenged from the city dump. Seven thousand newcomers were flocking into Santa Cruz each month. The government, which had cleared jungle for squatters to erect their shacks, sold two lots to the mission at a "giveaway price."

Two months after returning to Bolivia, the Watsons conducted an evangelistic campaign in an empty lot that served as a soccer field. Crowds gathered in spite of total lack of seats or platform. They also began a Sunday School in the crude schoolhouse. Three weekdays plus Sundays, Mom and Pop took the long local bus ride to conduct services and visit in every one of the 600 homes. Several residents knew the Lord or were interested in the gospel. Meanwhile a well was drilled and a simple shelter, a roof on two-by-fours without walls, was being erected. At Eastertime 1987, it was ready for occupancy. The work grew and the inhabitants of Villa Bolivia proudly spoke of "our church," even if they never attended.

A widow had heard the gospel 20 years previously from a SAM missionary. In Villa Bolivia she lived in a hovel, six by eight feet (1.8 by 2.4 m) with her three teen-age children. A young man soon took her daughter to live with him in another hovel. One son was "too simple to go into the army." His brother Abel collected fares on a city bus, working 16 hours a day for $2.50 (US) plus food. The mother had a cot; the boys slept on the floor. They had a table and two chairs. Outside they had three stones with a pot on top in which they cooked whatever food they could get. The mentally-underdeveloped son grew weaker and weaker on the scanty diet. Two weeks after meeting the family, the Watsons rented a vehicle and took the emaciated boy to a Christian doctor who provided some sample medicine, but gave a dim prognosis. The malnutrition had likely caused the brain deficiency and now, tuberculosis. A week later Abel sought out the Watsons in their apartment at 6:00 A.M. to report the death of his brother. A missionary friend drove the three of them to Villa Bolivia where the men took some of the boards intended for seats for the church, to construct a coffin. Men from the church helped dig the grave in the cemetery.

In August, construction began on a simple 30 by 60 foot (9 by 18 m) chapel: dirt floor, no windows or doors, just boards on blocks for pews, and a lean-to shelter behind for Sunday School classes. In October it was almost filled for an evangelistic campaign. Thirty-five people signed cards indicating a decision for Jesus Christ. Mom and Pop located over 30 of them in spite of lack of specific addresses, and spent hours discipling them in their own poor homes.

Business boomed for Elizabeth's correspondence course, especially since all candidates for baptism were required to complete the first course. In November, the first group of believers was baptized and the members joyfully celebrated the Lord's Supper. Abel had been baptized years before, when a child, by a pioneer missionary and now joined the new church.

Marcelo, a full-blooded Quechua Indian and a top seminary student, worked with them throughout the 1987 school year and then was called to pastor the new congregation, which consisted mostly of Quechua Indians.

Elizabeth planned to go to California alone to participate in her church's centennial, and 50th anniversary of their sending out their first missionary (herself). As the seminary year ended in November, Wilf's eyes gave out as he corrected piles of term papers, most written by hand, so they decided to travel together to:
>get his eye surgery (three weeks with the eye doctor);
>spend Christmas with Florence and family in Memphis. (Eric and wife Marge joined them; the entire family was together for the first time in 29 years);
>spend New Years in Texas with son, Eric;
>celebrate at Elizabeth's church in Oakland, California;
>get his new glasses after proper waiting period following surgery;
>return to Bolivia for the seminary opening in February.

It didn't leave much time for visiting friends!

Cataract surgery was successful. They returned to Bolivia for another year of teaching in the seminary and ministering with Pastor Marcelo in Villa Bolivia.

WEC asked them to again represent the mission, this time residing in Three Hills, Alberta where he had attended Prairie Bible Institute. Elizabeth was declared legally blind, but a quick laser zap restored her vision so both of them can drive. Wilf's carpal-tunnel syndrome and arthritis have also been healed. Now they're talking of short term visits to Mexico where WEC is opening up a work. Bob and Carol Evaul, who are directing SAM's Urban Bible Training Center, are urging them to return to teach a block of studies, knowing full well that there would be an uproar if Mom and Pop Watson were to teach at *their* school and didn't take their turn at CCC!

With genuine gratitude Wilfred and Elizabeth continue to receive and to give.

MEMORIES OF MY DAD by ERIC WATSON

My dad is the most GENEROUS man among mortals. He would receive gifts which I, even as a child, knew were to provide basic comforts, but he could see only the need of others. Surely the use of a needle and non-matching thread and an odd button would render the old suit coat that was four years past service, useful for six more months!

He was the QUIET DISCIPLINARIAN. Never did he raise his voice in anger while correcting his children. Containing his disappointment, he would pray that all would work for the best.

I saw his years of SACRIFICE and devotion to God's work. I not only saw but experienced the quiet tears inside when he had to send his children off to a foreign country to be taught by strangers. He wanted so much for them to have the educational opportunities that he had missed. He sacrificed normal family so that others could benefit from the mission that God had challenged the Rev. Wilfred T. Watson to do.

My father was also a BRAVE man. I know no other man who built wooden blocks to fit on the pedals of a Willis Jeep so his young son could reach the pedals to drive along the dry river bottoms during summer vacation. If a person in a ten mile radius of that old stump had not attended service last month, he would send his son out alone to gather up the "flock" and drive them to church. The next month people within the radius of a sonic boom would leave their homes before dawn to walk to church and be there two hours early. As a child I never understood why people would rather walk than ride to church. I guess if you considered him as a shepherd of the flock, then I was his "dingo" dog.

This man was also TOLERANT. He allowed his son to bring home a coyote, lynx, monkeys, parrots, rabbits, snakes, and normal cats. How many men lately have shuffled through a chicken house with his son's three hundred chickens to painstakenly place medicine with an eye dropper into a banty rooster that had been supposedly a fat broiler, and the boy had forgotten for a day or two to clean the floors? He did it knowing that if that one rooster died it would ruin his son's dream of becoming the Tyson Magnate of South America. Life sometimes hangs by a thread, and precariously depends on risking injury to one's self, slipping on an uncomfortable environment to keep a boy's dream alive.

Now the boy has grown into middle-aged manhood, but still has a child's wide-open eyes of wonderment at the SINGLE FOCUS that God placed on my father—to serve mankind and to learn internal peace with God and man.

I LOVE YOU, DAD.

EPILOGUE: SONSHIP, NOT SERVANTHOOD by WILFRED WATSON

I would like to close with some thoughts which sum up my life, Galatians 4:4-8:

> When the fullness of time was come, God sent his Son made of a woman, born under the law, that we might receive the adoption of sons. And because you are sons, God has sent forth the Spirit of His Son into your heart crying Abba, Father. [Note especially verse seven:] Wherefore you are no more a servant, but a son; and if a son, then an heir of God through Christ.

A son or a servant.

I'm so glad that in 1924 I became a son of God and I'm so glad that in 1992, after over 60 years in five countries of telling others about my Savior, preaching on the street corner in Calgary, pastoring, starting churches, and doing so many things that this book tells about, I'm so glad I'm still a son; I'm not a servant. I rejoice in my sonship, not in my service. As I used to sing at the Calgary Gospel Mission,

> Naught have I gotten, but what I received,
> Grace hath bestowed it since I have believed.
> Boasting excluded, pride I abase,
> I'm only a sinner, saved by grace.

We have been congratulated and praised for being missionaries for so long, but we *rejoice* in being sons.

A wealthy farmer had two sons. The younger, evil one, became a Christian. The elder, upright one remained a servant. The companion parable in the earlier part of Luke 15 closes with: "More joy shall be in heaven over one sinner that repents [that becomes a son] than over ninety and nine just persons who do not need repentance." They are servants.

These two groups, one with only one person and the other with ninety-nine, are represented by the two sons. One forfeited his right to sonship by taking his inheritance and running away and living riotously and, as his brother said, "spending his father's substance with harlots." We can stretch our imagination to what that boy did when he forfeited his sonship. Down amongst the pigs, hungry, he concluded, "The servants in my father's house eat better than I do. I'm going to return and say to my father, 'I'm no more worthy to be your son. Make me your servant.'" He rehearsed that speech over and over again, and when he came home he looked like the meanest of slaves: no shoes, tattered clothes, no ring. And he said, "I am no longer worthy to be called your son." He wasn't. There is no such thing as worthiness with grace.

The prodigal said, "I am no more worthy to be called your son." But he didn't get the words, "I would like to be called your servant," out of his mouth because his father responded with grace as our Father responds to us. God doesn't have servants. He only has sons and that's what we are.

The other boy, we forget about him. He was such a good boy, but he never got into the feast. I don't believe he represents saved people, but those who believe in good works and count on them for salvation. He said, "These many years do I serve you." He was a servant. In the spiritual sense he was not a son, but a servant.

That other rascal hoped that he could become a servant, but he never dreamed he might become a son. His father saw him in tatters and said, "Put on him the principal robe; make him look like a son."

Slaves don't have rings, but the father said, "Put the family ring on him; he is my son."

"As many as receive Him," says the Word of God, "to them he gives the power to become the sons of God" (John 1:12).

Slaves don't wear shoes; he didn't even have sandals. But the father said, "Put shoes on his feet; he's my son."

After more than 60 years of service, we don't consider ourselves servants; we are sons. And we stand before God exactly as we did in 1924, undone, no good, worthless. God saved us by grace and when we stand before Him, we're going to thank God for grace that made us a son, not a servant.

BIBLIOGRAPHY

BOOKS:

Anderson, Elof and Isabel: Hacaritama nd, np. (Covers the period of 1937-1977) Copyright by Elof Anderson.

Castilla F., Jorge: El Héroe Analfabeta. Cúcuta, Colombia: Librería "El Sembrador", 1983 pp 18, 19, 21-25.

Eley, Joan: God's Brumby: The Story of Joan Eley, Church-planter, Venezuela. From her personal diaries, Edited by Stewart Dinnen. Copyright Joan Eley, 1982. Cleveland, Qld 4163 Australia.

Muller, Sophie: Jungle Methods. New Tribes Mission, 1000 E. First Street, Sanford, FL. 32771, 1960. Copyright by Sophie Muller.

Ruscoe, A.W.: The Lame Take the Prey. Minneapolis, Minnesotas, Bethany Fellowship, Inc., 1968.

Savage, Stephen E.: Rejoicing in Christ, The Biography of Robert Carlton Savage. Reading, Vermont, Shadow Rock Press,1990. Copyright by S. E. Savage.

PERIODICALS:

"Anita" by Elizabeth Watson: Worldwide Thrust, Nov. 1970 pp 1-2.

"Camp Meeting Guahibo Style" by Wilf Watson: as above.

"Itinerario Teológico. La Mas Hermosa Aventura de Revelación y Descubrimiento" by Washington Padilla J.: Boletín Teológico, Fraternidad Teológica Latinoamericana, Tomo 18, No. 21-22, Junio 1986, pp 93,94. (Excerpt translated by Tait).

TRACTS:

"Four Things God Wants You to Know" Wheaton, IL, Good News Publishers. nd.

"4 Cosas que Usted Debe Saber" Medellín, Col., Tip. Union, nd (Spanish version of the above).

LETTERS:

From Wilfred Watson (collected by his Sunday School teacher, Lem Fowler since 1934, and by Mrs. Bobbie Johnstone since 1972) and from his friends, both personal and form, freely edited with approval from Wilfred Watson.

GLOSSARY

Acronyms:

CCC	Rural Training Center (Centro de Capacitación de Concepción)
PBI	Prairie Bible Institute
PRBI	Peace River Bible Institute
SAM	South America Mission
TEAM	The Evangelical Alliance Mission
WEC	Worldwide Evangelization Crusade

Phonetic Pronunciation Key:
    a, ä as in ma, pa
    e, ā as in say
    i, ē as in he
    o, ō as in go
    u, oo as in too
    ce, ci, s as in sāy, sēe
    ca, que, qui, co, cu, hard, as k
    ge, gi, h as in hāy, hēe
    ga, gue, gui, go, gu, hard as in gay, geese
    final s, as in lace, miss (no z sound)
    h, always silent

don, doña (dōn, dōnya): titles of respect used with first names.

Spanish names and places with an identifying phrase:

COLOMBIA

Aguilar, Luis. (ä guē lär', loo ēs'): Blacksmith in Gachalá
Alicia (älē'sēa): Colombian grandmother in Vancouver
Andrés (än dräs'): A lonely Christian
Aspasica (äs pä sē'cä): a mountain village north of Ocaña
Barranquilla (bä rän kē'yä): a Carribbean costal city
Betanla (bā tän'nyä): Chief Ramiri's village
Bogotá (bō gō tä'): the capital city
Bucaramanga (boo kä rä mäng'gä): a city
Buenaventura (bwä nä vän too' rä): a Pacific coast seaport
Corozal (cō rō säl'): a Piapoca village
Corozal, Anita (ä nē'tä): Infant with harelip and cleft palate

140 GLOSSARY

Cúcuta (coo'coo tä): City
Efigenia (ā fē hā'nyä): Mother of half of Marcos's children
El Anunciador (āl ä noon sēä dor'): The Announcer, a gospel launch
El Banco (āl bän'cō): a Magdalena river town
El Carmen (āl cär'mān): a liberal town
El Llanito (āl yä nē tō): Where Florence studied
Emanuel (ā män yoo āl'): WEC hospital in Bogotá
Emaús (ā mä oos'): Watsons' settlement with the Guajibos
Franco, Alicia (frän' cō, ālē'sēä): Daughter to Marcos and Rosa
Franco, Jorge Castilla, (Hōr'hā cäs tē' yä): Biographer, son of Marcos and Efigenia
Franco, Marcos (mär'cōs): Subsistence farmer in the Andes
Franco, Rosa: Franco's wife
Franco, Santander, (sän tän där'): Club-footed son of Rosa and Marcos
Fulano (foo lä'nō): An indefinite person as John Doe
Gaitán, Jorge Eliezar. (guy tän', hōr' hā ālē ā sär'): Mayor of Bogotá, assassinated April 9, 1948
Gonzalez (gōn sä'läs): Local politician
Guajibo (goo äh hē' bō): an Indian tribe of the plains
Julio (hoo'lē ō): Friend of Luis Agular, near Gachalá
La Donjuana (lä dōn hooä'nä): a small town; Wilf's first charge
La Gloria (lä glō'rē ä): a Port town on the Magdalena River
Marcelo (mär sä'lō): Student at Emaús; son of Chief Ramiri
Medellín (mā dā yēn'): a City
Mesa, Teo'filo (tā ō' fē lō): Elder in Cúcuta
Mitu (mē too'): a city
Moreno, Pedro (mō rā' nō, pā'drō): WEC pastor
Ocaña (ō cän' yä): a city
Padilla, Washington (pä dē lyä): a child in Bogotá
Pamplona (päm plō'nä): a town
Piapoca (pē ä pō'cä): An Indian tribe of the plains
Ramiri, (rä mē'rē): Christian Guajibo chief
Rico, Elias (ī cō, ā lē' äs): Elijah Rich, Christian peddler
Rio Negro (rē' ō nā' grō): Magdalena River town
Rodriguez, Pablo (rō drē'gās, pä' blo): Bible student from La Donjuana
Rojas-Pinilla (rō häs-pē nē lya): Colombian president
Salazar (sä lä sär'): a liberal town
Tirado, Constantino (tē rä' dō, cōn stän tē' nō), and Gloria: Colombians in Vancouver
Villavicencio (bē lyä vē sän'syō): the capital of El Meta state
Villavo (bē lyä' vō): a nickname for above.

GLOSSARY 141

VENEZUELA

Apure (ä poo'rä): river
Argenis (är hä'nēs): Dental Technician, became pastor of John 3:16 Church
Augusto (äoo goos' tō): Lay leader in Guasdualito
Barinas (bä rē' nës): City where the Watsons pastored
Barquisimeto (bär kē sē mä' tō): City where the Watsons pastored
Barrio Nuevo (bär' rēō nooē' vō): New suburb in Barquisimeto
El Habra (äl ä' brä): a desert village
Eriquito (ä rē kēë' tō): Nickname for Eric
Guaidí (gooó dē')(gwy dē'):a desert area
Guanare (guä nä'rä): State capitol
Guasdualito (gooäs dooälē' tō): Country area
Hilda (ēl' dä): Lay leader in Guaidi'
Juan Furia (hwän foo' rëä): A jungle area (see Pueblo Nuevo)
Julio (hoo' lēō): Pastor of Barrio Nuevo Church
Los Puertos (lōs pooär' tōs): Elizabeth's initial location
Los Ranchos (lōs rän' chōs): Desert village
Maracaibo (mä rä k bō): TEAM headquarters city; also a lake
Pueblo de Dios (pwä' blō dä dēōs'): Village of God, new name for Juan Furia
Pueblo Nuevo (pooä' blō nooä' vō): Other new name for Juan Furia
Rubio (roo' bēō): Where Florence attended TEAM school

BOLIVIA

Abel (ä bäl'): Widow's son in Villa Bolivia
Aguilar, Walter and Aurora (äguē lär', walter, äoo rō' rä): Christians in Pailón
Arandia, Julio and Eulalia,(är än' dëä, hoo' lēō, äool ä' lëä): students at first CCC, from Pailón
Bravo, Luis,(brä' vō, loo ēs'): Pastor in San José de Chiquitos
Centro de Capacitación Cristiana (sän' trō dä cä pä sē tä sē ōn' krēs tē ä' nä): Christian Opportunity Center, in Concepción (CCC)
Chávez, Augusto (chä' väs, äoo goos' tō): SAM pastor, church leader
Chochis (chō' chēs): a town near Brazil
Cochabamba (cō chä bäm' bä): City where Seatons lived in 1984
Concepción (cōn säp sēōn'): Conception. Town where the CCC was held.
Escobar, Carmelo,(äs cō bär', cär mä' lō): School teacher in Pailón
Fortín Suárez Arana (fōr tēn' sooä' räs ärä' nä): Army base in eastern Bolivia
Julio (hoo'lēō): Christian in Pailón and Paraíso
Marcelo (mär sä' lō): Seminarian who replaced Watsons in Villa Bolivia
Pailón (pó lōn'): a railroad town
Paraíso (pä raē ' sō): Paradise. A miserable area for homesteaders
Pozo Verde (pōsō vär' dä): Indian village near Pailón
Robaré (rō bä rä'):a town

142 GLOSSARY

San Ignacio (sän ēg nä′ sē ō): Midpoint on road from San José to CCC
San José de Chiquitos (sän hō sā′ dā chē kē′ tōs): Saint Joseph of the small ones. Town so named because of the diminutive Indians.
Sandoval (sän dō väl′): Town near the Brazilian border
Santa Cruz (sän tä croos′): State and state capital
Santiago Sierra (sän tē ā′ gō sē är′ rä): A mountain range
Villa Bolivia (bē′ lyā bō lē′ vē ä): A shanty-town on the edge of Santa Cruz.

Alberta

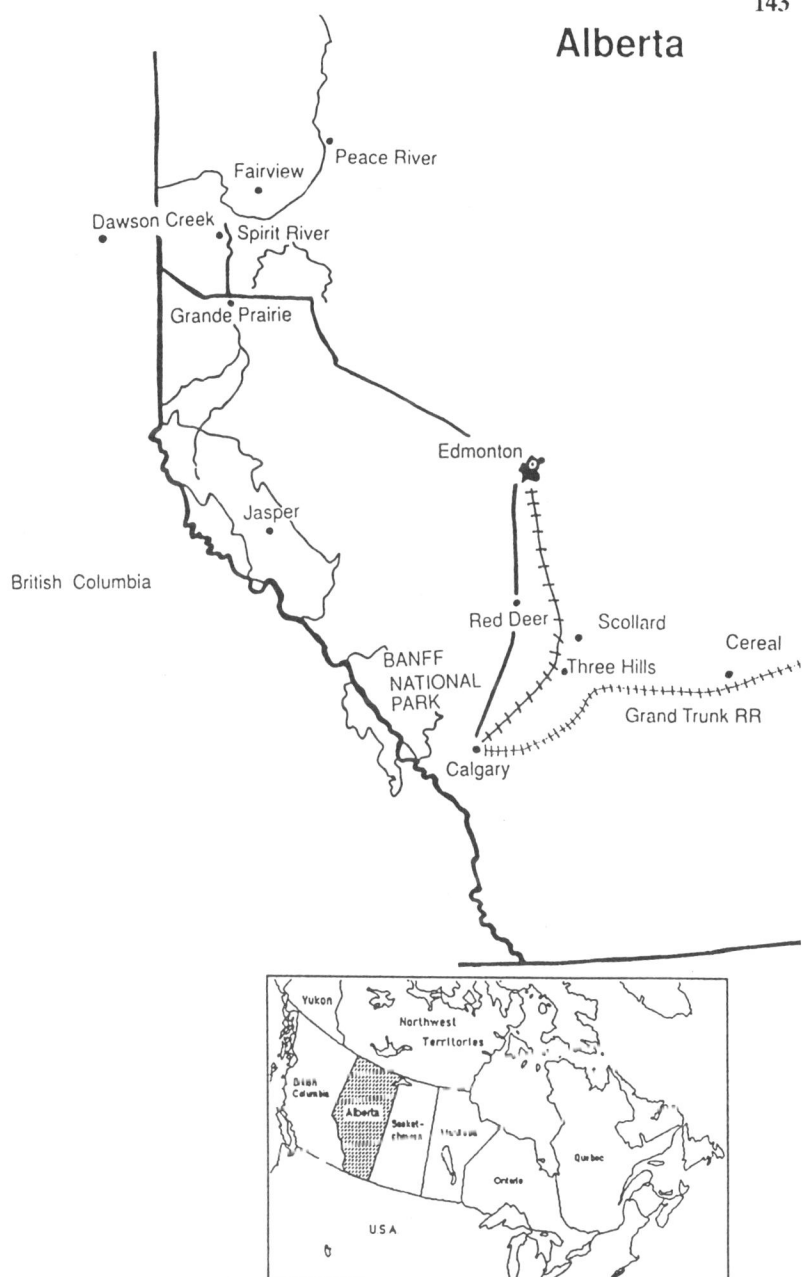

Map of Alberta, Canada

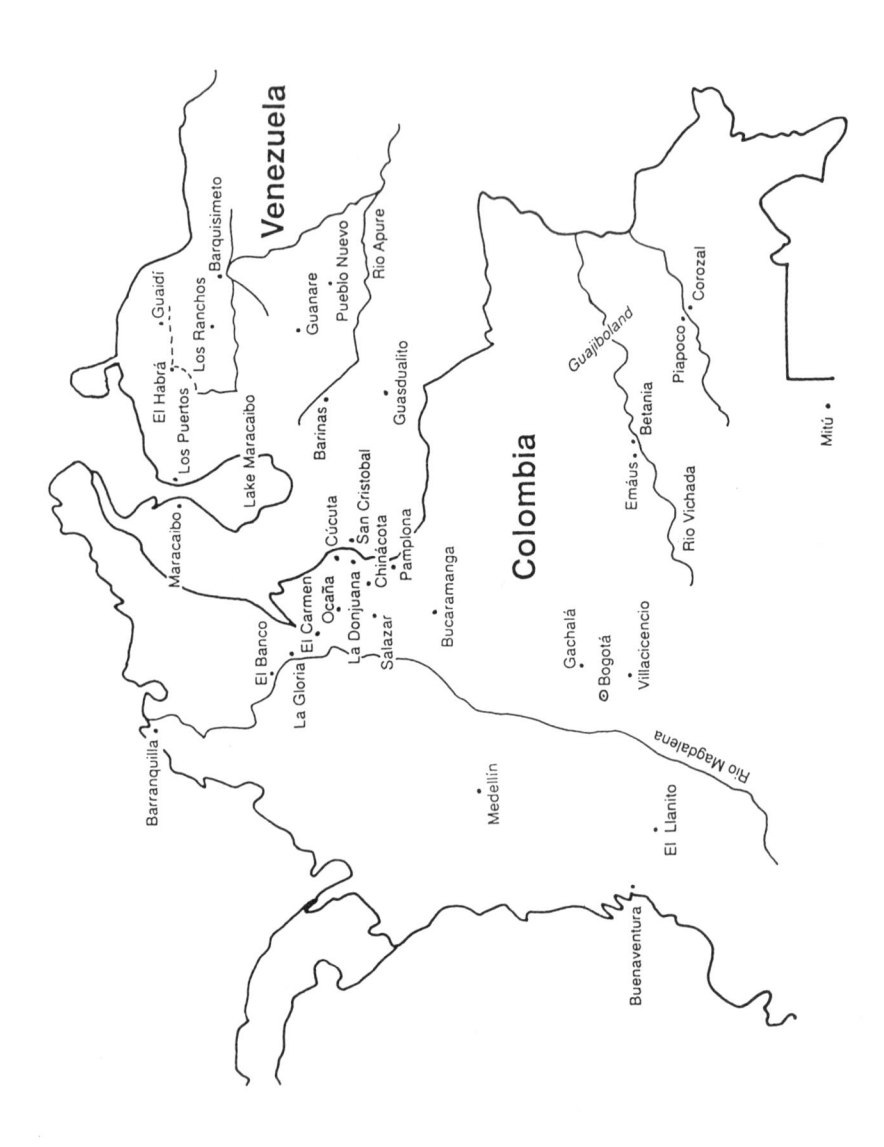

Map of Colombia and Venezuela

Bolivia

Concepción • San Ignacio
• Cochabamba Santa Cruz   San José de Chiquitos
            Pailon   Chochis
                           • Santiago
                       Robore

Colombia
Venezuela
Bolivia

South America

Map of Bolivia and South America

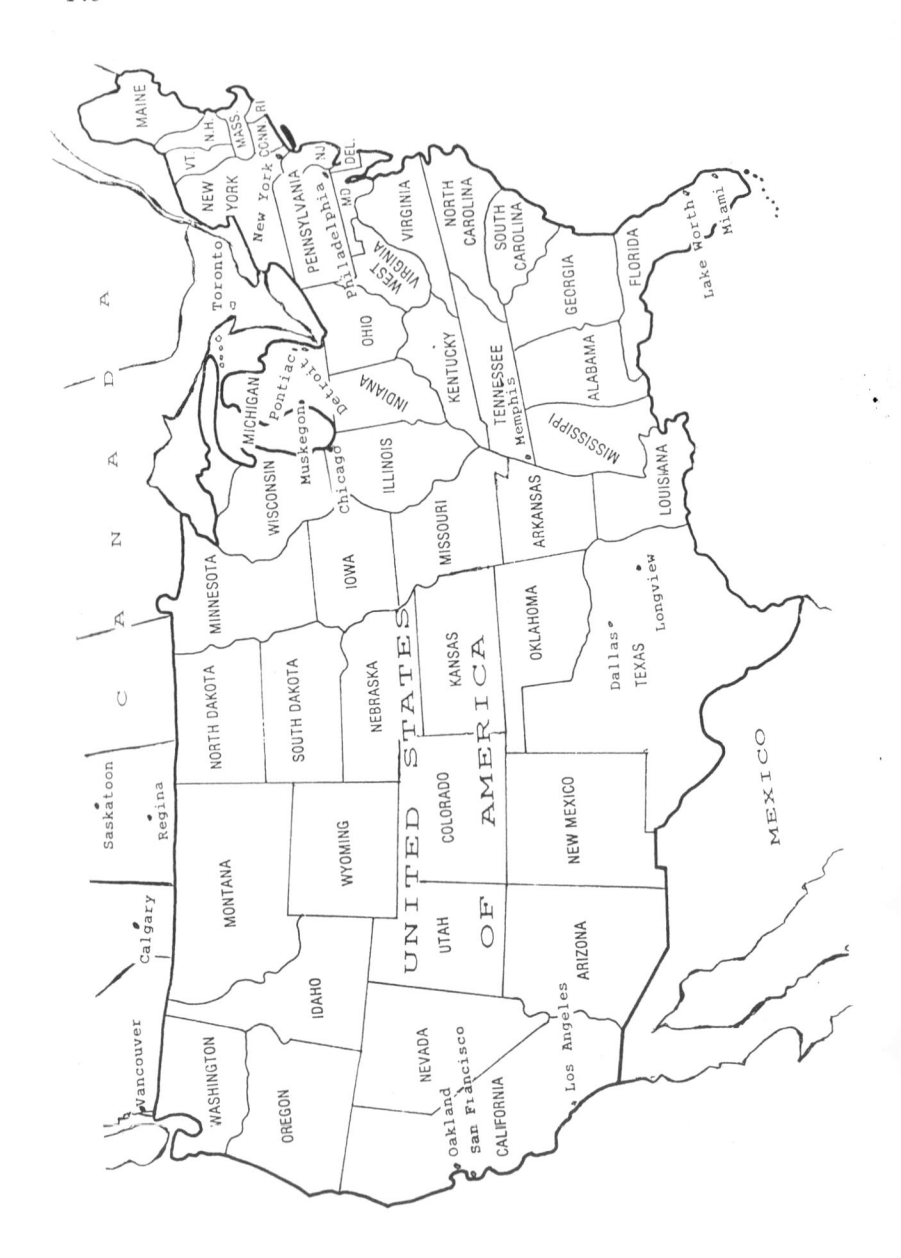

Map of The United States